SHE RISES
for tomorrow

FEMALE ENTREPRENEURS WHO BROUGHT IDEAS TO LIFE AND INSPIRE THE WORLD

VOLUME 3

NAYIA PIERRAKOS

ISBN: 978-0-6452420-7-2

Disclaimer

This anthology is a memoir. It reflects the authors' present recollections of experiences over time. Some names and characteristics have been changed, some events have been compressed, and some dialogue has been recreated.

CONTENTS

INTRODUCTION

Hi, my name is Kimmie Wong. I am an entrepreneur, wife, and mother of three beautiful children. After being stuck in a corporate job for many years, I felt completely unfulfilled. I knew there was more to life than the normal nine-to-five grind. I had many dreams and business ideas I wanted to bring to life. Before finally stepping out of the corporate world, I had many failed attempts.

Yes, there were some days I felt hopeless and even miserable. I was unsure of what I truly wanted to dedicate my life to, I only knew I didn't want to spend it on someone else's watch. Despite many hurdles and obstacles along the way, I found my true passion as a successful publicist and marketing strategist.

Now, I am my own boss. I have the freedom to live a balanced lifestyle. Having more time to spend with my family and dedicate to the things I love has brought me so much joy and fulfillment.

Throughout my coaching career, I've spoken to many women—women who feel stuck in their daily routines while experiencing extreme pressures from society. Even though these women have incredible ideas and dreams, they just cannot seem to make those dreams come true.

There are countless strong, smart women who want to rediscover their purpose, pursue their calling, and start a business, but who face many roadblocks along the way that make them feel as if they aren't cut out for the world of entrepreneurship. Many of these women were on the verge of giving up and giving in to a life they did not really want. I resonate wholeheartedly with these women; it was as if they mirrored my own past journey.

What makes me hopeful for women's futures and their endless career opportunities? It is the fact that I've also met incredible women who have endured just as much—brave women who took the leap and the risk to follow their dreams. Some of these incredible women are featured in this book.

They share their stories with you, the women of the future, because they want to inspire you. The women in these chapters are all entrepreneurs from around the world. Even though they come from different backgrounds, the message is simple: Their powerful stories of how they brought their ideas to life will ignite the female entrepreneurs of tomorrow.

I invited these women to contribute to this book to create a powerful sense of togetherness among women. Standing as one, we are strong. When we collaborate, we are an unstoppable force.

If you've ever felt like your ideas aren't being heard, if the road to success seems too difficult, then these pages will show you're not alone. There are women who have walked this path before you and they all share their stories in this collective tell-all book.

This book will empower those women who have lost faith in their own abilities to continue their path—to stand back up when they've been knocked down by life's obstacles and keep pursuing their dreams. Reading their stories will reignite the fire within you and sustain you on your journey.

If they did it, so can you.

When She Rises, She Rises with Tomorrow in mind. Even though she can't see what the future holds, she knows if she takes action now there will be a positive outcome in the future. Her ideas and dreams will manifest into reality, and it all starts with her determination to rise!

Kimmie Wong
Founder and Publisher
She Rises for Tomorrow books

Would you like to elevate your personal brand and have your message reach millions?

Visit
www.kimmiewong.com

*You are the architect
of your life.*

Nayia Pierrakos

"You are Spartan. You are of great courage and strength because that is your lineage." My mother instilled this in me from a very young age. Ancient Sparta is one of the most well-known cities in Classical Greece, known for its highly skilled warriors and its reverence for stoicism. When my mother brought my siblings and me to the U.S. from Greece, I held tight to this knowledge of where I came from, and the strength of my roots, and the Spartan identity that gave me the courage to fight for myself.

It was July 20, 1988. I was eleven years old when we left our home of Skala Laconia and everything we knew for what my parents promised would be a better life in America.

In the beginning when we first came to the US, it was everything but that better life. On September 6 of that year, I was thrown into sixth grade with no choice but to figure out how to survive in my new environment. That first year was grueling but I got through it. I learned the language, excelled in academics and became the first person in my family to graduate college.

I felt all grown up after graduation. I was paying my own bills and becoming responsible for myself. But I was working in a job that I didn't enjoy. I felt like my fate was not in my hands, that my future was being determined by others. So, I decided to take back control of my life and start my own business.

With my mother's help, I opened my first little kiosk at a local mall selling designer accessories and sunglasses. Within a few years I was growing so quickly and had more money coming in than I knew what to do with. One day, a local realtor recommended I start investing in real estate, and before I knew it, I had my real estate license.

In 2002 I got married. My husband (at the time) and I built a custom home. We were on top of the world! My retail business was growing. I expanded to more locations and increased my product lines. Financially, things were going great. I was making six figures in my mid-twenties! I started buying rental properties and real estate was appreciating like crazy at an annual rate of 20% per year.

During this time, I welcomed my first son into the world in 2005, and in 2007 my second son. My husband and I then decided that it was time for me to sell my retail business and become a stay-at-home mom. We went from having two incomes to just my husband's salary. Everything was going just as we had planned. My husband's job was going well; he was a top producer at work, and he was making more than enough to support us. We had two beautiful little boys and we were living in our amazing dream home.

And then, 2008 came around. The economy crashed. My husband was laid off. I was pregnant again, expecting our third son. We knew we had to act. We had a family to support and decisions had to be made. The Spartan in me had to come out and help fight for my family. We could not let the fear of losing our home and everything we had worked for paralyze us.

We went to a franchise expo, hoping that this would solve our problems. Franchises have a proven system, after all. We can't fail, we thought. An opportunity presented itself: a local franchise only fifteen minutes from our home. Wow! We felt so lucky! We invested over $100k and took out loans to buy the business. We were certain it would be a success.

It took us six months to realize that we were digging ourselves in a deep, dark hole. We had been so busy running the day-to-day operation, working twelve to fifteen-hour days, that we didn't realize we were losing money. The business was costing more money than it was making every month. We hadn't done our due diligence prior to purchasing it. It was a painful lesson learned the hard way. We could not afford to keep it. And things kept going downhill for us.

On a chilly afternoon on October 28 2010, I walked into my home and found my mother-in-law on the kitchen floor. I thought she had just fainted. Aristotle, my eighteen-month-old, had fallen asleep on his high chair with one leg out. He had been trying to get out since his Yiayia ("grandma" in Greek) had finished feeding him lunch and collapsed in front of him hours ago. I froze at the sight! My first thought was, where is Georgio, my five-year-old? I called out his name in sheer panic. He answered, "Mom, I'm upstairs. I was sleeping." He'd thought his Yiayia was sleeping on the floor, and he didn't want to wake her. My mind was racing. What if I had got home at 6pm that evening like I normally did? What could have happened? Two small kids all alone. That day was a turning point for us, requiring unimaginable adjustments in our lives.

After my mother-in-law's passing, the recession of 2009, and the real estate crash, I fell into a deep depression. It was hard to see how we were going to make it. We continued to struggle with our franchise business which was still costing more than it was making. We couldn't afford daycare for the boys. To top it off, real estate had decreased in value by more than 50% in my area and my investment properties were worth less than what I had paid for them.

I remember paying our mortgage with a credit card for over six months until the card hit its limit. We started receiving foreclosure notices and an auction date was set. Our home was now worth $200K less than what we had paid for it. We needed help fast, so we decided to short-sale our dream home to help save our business. It was a painful decision, but as a real estate agent I knew how this worked.

We rented a small townhouse where I had to carry groceries and a toddler up four flights of stairs. I had to constantly tell three little boys under the age of seven to be quiet so our lower-level neighbor would not complain about the noise. This was not what we had dreamed of. It had all gone so wrong.

A constant nightmare played in my mind for months: the memory of losing my mother-in-law, our home, the fear of losing our business and all the money and time we had invested. Soon I could not take it anymore. I felt like I had lost everything, even my identity. It was as if I had forgotten how to fight and stand up for myself. Finally, anger kicked in. What am I doing? What is wrong with me? I asked myself. This is not who I am! I was sick and tired of feeling sorry for myself! I had to do something. I turned to God, begging for help and asking for a sign. From the age of twelve I had learned that if I asked God for a sign, I would get one. I had just forgotten to ask.

It was during this time that I came across the book *The Secret* by Rhonda Byrne. I would listen to the audio book every day. It became an obsession. I learned about the law of attraction and how our thoughts can create what we desire and ultimately help us change our life and our reality. It was the one thing that was distracting me from the nightmare I kept replaying in my mind.

I began putting the suggestions and practices of the book into use.

Let's play a game, I would tell myself.

I would focus on something positive, a person with certain skills for example, and within two days someone with those skills would show up to offer help in our business. It was phenomenal! I kept this newfound secret to myself. I didn't want anyone to tell me it was not real, that things were just a coincidence, or that I was crazy. I knew deep down that I was doing my part in creating my life.

The synchronicities, or "signs", continued. I started feeling that I had some control over my life again. I asked my friend Dara if she knew anyone doing well in real estate investing and she connected me to Dave. He was flipping properties in an area one hour away from where I lived. All three of us met for coffee one morning and we got on the topic of our favorite books. He mentioned *Think and Grow Rich* by Napoleon Hill. I reached inside my purse and pulled out a copy of the exact book. We hit it off immediately. I seized the opportunity and asked to meet him once a week, follow him around, and work for free as his assistant.

"I just want to learn," I said. He said yes and I was so excited!

I would drop off the boys at daycare once a week and make the hour-long drive to learn about renovating houses. That experience took the fear away!

I saw houses with termite damage, structural damage, fire, mold, you name it. I learned that it can all be fixed when you know what you are doing and have the right systems and people in place. I took a $25K credit card with a 0% offer and invested it with Dave on my first renovation deal. Within four months I got my money back to pay off the credit card and made a $9,500 profit. It felt amazing!

After that year, I was ready to start renovating houses. One of my first deals was in a gated community. It was a bank owned property and a pipe had burst. Water was leaking down to the basement from the second floor and mold was growing. I was not deterred or afraid to tackle this. Dave and I knew what to do.

We made an offer on the house for $100K less than the asking price, knowing that the bank would not want to deal with the damages to the house. We were not afraid of the work ahead of us. The bank accepted our offer. The house needed around $60K in repairs to replace the kitchen, hardwood floors, renovate a bathroom, and remediate the mold. After closing costs, real estate commissions, and paying hard money lenders we sold that property and walked away with a $70K profit in less than six months.

I learned a lot working with Dave! Not only what to do, but also what not to do by observing his mistakes. I also learned about the risks involved.

When renovating properties, I had to use hard money lenders, sign personal guarantees, and list all my assets. All this made me extremely uncomfortable. The recession was still fresh in my mind, and I feared that the market could turn again.

In 2012 my fears almost came to fruition.

I started a condo conversation with two partners in Washington DC. We had estimated that we were going to make a total profit of $300K in six months. What should have been the best deal of my life turned out to be my biggest nightmare. Anything and everything that could go wrong did go wrong. We had issues with contractors not showing up or using materials that were not to code. We had issues with permits and delays. We had to fire our first contractor and raise money from our friends and family to pay someone else to finish the project.

What should have been a six-month project turned into an eighteen-month nightmare. I worried that I would have to sell my rentals to pay off the private lenders I had borrowed money from to do this deal. It took me eighteen months to get out of this horrific situation. I ended up making a $2,000 profit on the project and, luckily, did not have to dissolve any of my other assets. I was so relieved! It was, by far, one of the biggest lessons of my real estate career.

As the saying goes, "When the student is ready, the teacher appears."

I knew there had to be other ways to buy, but what were they?

In February 2013, I was at an event in NJ when I met Keith. Keith was attending the event all the way from Texas. We talked about our real estate business and the strategies we were using. That is when Keith mentioned, I buy houses "subject-to" the existing loan.

"What? Is that even possible?" I asked.

"Yes", he replied and explained to me how it can be done.

Buying a property "subject-to" the existing loan means that the seller keeps the loan in their name and you commit to making continued payments on that loan. In return, the seller signs over the deed or ownership to the buyer. So, the seller gets a quick and easy solution and they get to move on with their life, and the buyer gets a good deal on an investment property without needing to take out a loan from a bank. I knew I had found my answer!

A month later I was at a local real estate meetup. Everyone introduced themselves by saying what they specialized in. A guy in the back of the room stood up and said, "I buy houses creatively using subject-to". I immediately turned around, pointed at him and quietly said, "I need to talk to you."

Joe was super nice. I hadn't met anyone in my area that knew how to put creative deals like that together. I decided to ask for his help. I asked if Joe would be willing to help me structure a deal if I brought it to him. He said yes! This was it! I knew it would only be a matter of time before I had a deal. I was super excited for what was to come. I had an internal knowing that a deal was around the corner.

Within three weeks, I had a lead come in from Craigslist that met the criteria I was looking for. I called Joe and we scheduled an appointment with the seller. We met with the seller and were able to structure a win-win "subject-to" creative deal on my first appointment. The property had a fair market value of $375K, had a loan on it for $325K, and with Joe's help I was able to buy it three weeks later for only $4,682.61 out of pocket. I could not believe it! I purchased a property for less than

$5,000 that only needed a new coat of paint and a few closet doors. Joe helped me structure that deal in such a way that I was able to solve the seller's problem: they were purchasing another house but could not afford two mortgages. I was able to bring value to the seller, create win-win results, and I would make a profit without having to use a lot of capital upfront, get a loan, or use hard money lenders. I knew this was the solution I had been looking for. A way to buy real estate without having to borrow money. I felt like I won the lottery! Two years later I sold the property and made a $75K profit.

Joe told me that he had learned this strategy from his mentor, Mario. So, I bought a ticket to Mario's next training event in Chicago. On October 2, 2013 I signed an agreement and paid $20K to work with Mario and his team for one year. I made up my mind that if Keith and Joe could do this business, so could I. I was going to make it work no matter what.

Eighteen months later another door opened for me. Mario saw the success I was having and brought me onboard as a coach on his team. I was the only woman and the youngest coach he had in his organization. This opportunity enabled me to teach others how to become successful in real estate investing. I traveled around the country and spoke to large audiences of real estate investors. I coached hundreds of investors from all over the United States, analyzed thousands of deals, and helped my students structure hundreds of profitable deals.

While I was doing great, I was not seeing others produce the results I was. One of the biggest challenges as a coach and mentor was to see my students and clients quit and give up on themselves. My desire for their success was stronger than theirs. This was hard for me to accept, as I wanted to help them all succeed. I felt that Mario's training program needed more components so I branched off on my own and developed my own unique training strategy. In order to guarantee success for my clients, I introduced personal development into real estate. It was about more than just investing in real estate for me. It was about overcoming one's personal limiting beliefs and patterns, and showing people how to improve their lives in practical ways while using real estate as the vehicle to create financial freedom.

My purpose and mission in life is to improve the lives of others through my courses and training and help make 1,000 millionaires. We all want to help others but unless we have the ability and means to help ourselves first, we won't be able to make the impact we want. To date, I have personally purchased and sold over $25,000,000 of residential real estate. I have helped build a village in Haiti, granted scholarships, and helped numerous non-profit organizations.

It's my passion to be a catalyst and an example for others in helping them create their best life. Success is a team sport. No one can become successful alone without the support of others. We all know what we know until we learn something new. We have to seek knowledge and education from people who have what we want and have been where we are, then apply the training in order to build our own experience and reach our next step of the journey. This is what I have done, and what I strive to do for others.

• • •

You know a lot more than you think you know, and you have achieved more than you give yourself credit for. Know that the more pressure that's put on you the more beautiful you become. Just like the pressure put on a diamond.

If you want your life to change, then you have to change some of the things you are doing in your life.

It is the secret of the law of attraction. If you can imagine it, you can get it. It is possible! It starts with faith. If someone can do it, you can do it. If I can do it, you can do it!

Just like Napoleon Hill said: "Whatever the mind of man can conceive and believe, it can achieve."

My life may not look like I thought it would when I first started, but it is so much more than I could have expected! You are a creator, and you have the power to make changes that will improve your life. You have the ability to co-create an amazing life, whether in a relationship with someone you love, or in a business partnership. Now, let's go co-create with God and each other.

I believe in you!

Nayia Pierrakos

NAYIA PIERRAKOS

Originally from Greece, Nayia came to America in 1988. An entrepreneur since her early twenties, Nayia has broad experience from the retail, recruiting, consulting, and real estate industries.

Nayia purchased her first property twenty years ago when she was twenty-three. Nayia loves to learn and has a student mindset, and she has used this passion for growth to find ways to help others become the architects of their lives. She is achieving this through her company

Wealth Thru Real Estate where she educates individuals who want to use real estate as the vehicle to become financially independent.

Nayia is also a Co-Founder of My Deal Mind, a software utility company providing all the tools and resources real estate investors need.

Nayia's mission is to help make 1,000 millionaires.

Her biggest accomplishment is being a mom of three amazing boys, Georgio, Vasili, and Aristotle. She wants to set a good example and make them proud so they can create their best life.

INVITATION FROM THE AUTHOR

Visit our website and discover the many resources available to help you create your best life, both personally and financially:

www.WealthThruRE.com

CONNECT WITH THE AUTHOR

Business Name: Wealth Thru Real Estate
Website: www.WealththruRE.com
Facebook: www.facebook.com/wealthrure
Email: Nayia@WeaththruRE.com

It is in our darkest moments that we must begin to focus to see the light.

Aishah Tatum

It was the first day of January 2014, around 10 a.m. The howling wind brushed against the window and woke me up out of my sleep. My heart was heavy and my spirit burdened because I knew I was making a mistake. The night before I met up with my ex-boyfriend to "hang out". We had been together for four long, emotionally draining, and painful years.

Out of loneliness and sadness, I called him. We had been stuck in a cycle of breaking up to make up and I grew comfortable with the pattern. That night, I was to attend a friend's wedding reception and I didn't want to go alone. We danced, had a good time, but deep down inside I knew we didn't belong together. My friend walked over to me and told me how good we looked together and that she was happy for me. Little did she know how unhappy I truly was.

Once I graduated from college, my life was in no way how I'd imagined it. I was working a job that drained me. The day to day commute, micromanagement and sales quotas made me feel like I was living in a cage with no way out. I was inspiring students to continue their education beyond high school, set goals for themselves and plan for their future, which gave me satisfaction. But deep down inside I knew there was more to life. I was tired of working check to check.

I woke up to that howling wind, put my feet on the soft floor and sat on the side of the bed. I started to feel a deep inner pain, like I was letting myself down once again. I walked to the bathroom and couldn't look myself in the eyes. I thought, how could I do this to myself again? Those positive statements I wrote on the mirror all seemed like lies. As I glanced at them one by one—I am beautiful, I am happy, I love myself—I thought to myself, yeah right, what a bunch of B.S. After years of living with low self-esteem and being in yet another toxic relationship, I couldn't recognize myself anymore.

After brushing my teeth, I went out to the living room and saw my beautiful mother sitting at her computer typing away. She heard me and said in a soft and loving voice, "Good morning, my beautiful daughter." I smiled and walked up to her slowly and put my arm around her. As she turned to look at me, she said, "Aishah, I really hope you leave him alone. He's no good for you."

My mother then gave me a big hug and told me to check my email. The first email was a speaker opportunity. I became nervous at the thought of applying. So, I ignored it and went on to the next one. The truth was, I just didn't think I was good enough and I feared rejection. The other email was from my mother, a poem that read, "No matter what this year brings, may you be happy, find joy and live your dreams." She was always pushing me to get out of my own way, believe in myself and live my dreams.

Two weeks later, I was sitting in a high school parking lot in my black mustang completing work notes. My phone rang and I looked down to see that it was my mother. She would call me every day to check on me and always had something positive to say. I answered the phone, "Hey, Mom." She said, "Aishah, the doctor ran some tests, and wants to refer me to an oncologist." I felt my heart skipping beats. Time stopped. I closed my eyes, put a hand on my forehead and took a breath.

For months my mother had been complaining of abdominal pain off and on. We went to the hospital and the doctor advised her that she had diverticulitis. They prescribed medication and sent us home.

I was now in panic mode, thoughts racing and breathing rapidly. I'd heard of the word before, but I couldn't remember what it meant. I just knew it wasn't good. I told my mother I was heading home and would be there soon. Immediately upon hanging up, I googled the word and I stared at the screen in disbelief.

A cancer doctor, I thought, this can't be! My mother had assured me that the doctor didn't think she had cancer but based on her test results she wanted her to see a specialist. We met with the specialist who scheduled a surgery. He assured us in the meeting that it would be a quick procedure and not to worry.

On the day of the surgery, my brother, aunt and I all went along. We waited with our mother, cracking jokes and laughing until they called her in. We all said a prayer as they rolled my mother away. I couldn't help but stare at the clock. Hours passed. We were expecting a three-hour surgery, but several hours had gone by with no word. I knew something was wrong.

Eventually, the doctor called us to the consultation room. We sat on the edge of our seats. I blurted out, "Is my mom okay?" He replied, "Yes, the surgery went well. Your mother is in recovery. However, we did find cancer."

I began to cry. I couldn't believe what I was hearing. My mother was a vegetarian and lived an active lifestyle. How could this be? The doctor then advised us that it was a rare form of cancer that only impacts 1% of the population, so they had very little treatment options available. He advised that my mother could try a certain type of chemotherapy, which he felt would be beneficial. My brother and I then spent hours searching to find alternative options for treatment, and bought books looking for ways to help. We learned about alternative methods of healing, holistic nutrition, ozone therapy and even a place in Mexico that used apricot seeds to reverse the disease.

A few weeks later, I was suddenly called into the office at work after finishing a presentation at a local high school. As soon as I walked into the office my immediate supervisor said, "Aishah, I'm sorry to inform you that today is your last day." I was both in shock and in a state of relief. I was tired of being micromanaged and conducting scripted presentations that promoted the school I worked for. The cost of admission was too high and the amount of money the graduates would earn was not commensurate; it seemed like a rip off. A few days later my then boyfriend and I broke up again.

I was an emotional wreck, and I spiraled into a depression. I was unhappy with my life, income, my body, and myself. I felt like I was living in the twilight zone. I was watching my mother fight for her life, yet at the same time she was continuing to pursue her dreams of acting and comedy.

Over the next few months my mother's condition improved. It improved so much that we almost forgot she had cancer. My mother went in for a scan and they told her that she was doing amazing. They didn't detect the cancer in her body.

Just as she always had, my mother was encouraging me to go after my dreams. She told me that if I really wanted to speak and write then I should start. I decided to go for it. Within one week, I wrote my first book, *The Fearless Woman*, in honor of my mom, the most fearless woman that I know. My mother was an actress and an author, and she was running after her dreams!

We would go to different comedy clubs and I would sit in awe as my mother got on stage to perform jokes. She lit up a whole room. We would go dancing and the entire floor would stare in admiration. We decided to put together a stage play to bring one of her books to life.

One day, we were sitting in the living room watching a lifetime movie, one of our favorite things to do, and my mother said, "Aishah, come here." She then placed my hand on her stomach and we both looked at each other and knew something was wrong.

I felt a sharp pain in the pit of my stomach. My mother went in to see the doctor later that week to get a scan. There were now six tumors covering her abdomen and back. My mother had been on chemo for months and it had done nothing.

The doctor scheduled another surgery and this time my mother didn't recover as well. After a few weeks, she was discharged from the hospital and the plans we had to put on the stage play were put on hold. It was extremely difficult watching her struggle to regain her strength, but she began making progress.

A few weeks later she emailed me an opportunity to speak and be featured in a magazine and I jumped on it. I was so excited! A month later, I was on stage speaking, and when I finished I received a standing ovation. My confidence increased drastically and I knew I had the "it" factor.

Then my ex and I got back together. He was the first and only man I'd ever been with. When he called telling me he loved me and wanted to work it out, I went back to him. It was like he had a hold on me.

A week later, my mother sought the opinion of another doctor and, looking back, I wish she hadn't. When my mother came home from the doctor, she lay down on the couch and refused to get up. Her drive to fight was gone. I asked my brother what had happened, and he said, "The doctor told mom he was surprised that she was still alive based on her condition and wanted to shake her hand."

I couldn't believe it! How dare he say that to my mother! Those words destroyed her spirit. The next several weeks were painful, as my mother struggled to walk to the bathroom. She was in so much pain that we had to give her CBD oil so she could sleep. I was still holding on to hope, thinking that my mother could make it. However, she no longer had an appetite, stopped speaking and wanted to sleep all day. It was the most emotionally painful and challenging experience of my life to watch my mother, my hero, begin to wither away.

My brother found a place in Mexico that might be able to help. Our uncle flew all of us there. The whole way I prayed, begging God for a miracle. After running a few tests and doing lab work, they called us into the office, telling us that they had never seen anything like it before. The tumor was growing so fast that it was crushing my mother's kidneys. They told us, "We're sorry, there is nothing that we can do."

On December 10 2014 I laid in bed with my mother knowing it would be the last time I would hold her. I took her soft and warm hands in mine and wanted so desperately for her to look me in my eyes, and to hear her voice. But she could no longer speak or see, as her body began shutting down. But I knew that she could still hear me. I whispered in my mother's ear and told her how proud of her I was, how much I loved her and that she was my hero. I reminisced on the time she taught me how to tie my shoes, how she had always been there for me, taking pictures of me at my prom, high school graduation and college commencement ceremony, cheering me on.

December 10 was the day my mother took her last breath.

I didn't know what or how to feel after losing my mother. Her sudden absence was so surreal. I thought I was in a bad dream and needed to wake up, but couldn't. I was empty, and I felt like someone had taken a shotgun and blown my heart wide open. I fell into shock.

Three days after arriving back in Atlanta, I called my boyfriend to talk to him about how I was feeling. In response, he said, "Aishah, you need to move on with your life." I knew there was someone else again. My mother had been gone for three days, and he dumped me. I hung up the phone and sat in the bathroom for hours. It was in those moments that I contemplated taking my own life. I didn't want to live.

I was broke, broken, and devastated. I cried endlessly. I yelled at God, "How could you do this? My mother was a good person, she didn't deserve that! I still need her! Why did you take her from me?" I worked myself up until it was hard to breathe. My older brother, Iman called me and told me he wanted me to move in with him for as long as I needed.

A week later my ex called begging me to take him back and I finally had the courage to say no and mean it. My mother had asked me to promise her that I wouldn't marry him. I realized that I really did deserve better. The next several months were hard—getting out of bed, brushing my teeth and even eating all seemed daunting. I had no desire to do anything.

My brother helped me get to a place where I could finally start moving forward with my life. He put me through an IT training program so that I could start earning money and getting out of the house. The IT program allowed me to start consulting at hospitals and clinics nation-wide. It was great money but required eighty-four hours a week of work. It kept my mind off the pain I was feeling.

After speaking with a friend, I decided to start therapy. It was so helpful just to talk to someone who didn't know me, wouldn't judge me, and who could offer insight. After several sessions, I realized there was something deeper that wasn't being addressed.

I was starting to feel unfulfilled and empty in my job. One day, I was flicking through TV channels and Tyler Perry's *A Family that Preys* was on. I went into a trance. Flashbacks of my mother and I sitting in the theater began playing in my mind. I remembered the credits rolling and my mother holding my hand, looking me in my eyes and singing to me, "Aishah, if you get the chance to dance, I hope you dance."

I realized then that I had been running away from my life and all the pain, trying to block it the best way I knew how. In the process, I was getting further and further away from my purpose. I knew in that moment I had to make a decision—I could stay in my pain or I could pursue the purpose God had for me. I chose to pursue my purpose, but I knew I still needed to heal first. I prayed to God to help me because I had nowhere else to turn.

My mother had been my rock and now I had to learn how to rely on God and myself to get me through. Almost a year from the day of my mother's passing, I found a school in Atlanta called The Living Foods Institute. It was founded by a woman who had been diagnosed with both breast and cervical cancer at the same time. She reversed both within six months without chemotherapy, radiation, or surgery. I was intrigued and knew in my soul that was where I needed to go.

I called the school a week later and applied to attend. I wanted to learn how to heal holistically. During the program I learned how to heal the body with living foods, essential oils, supplements, subconscious reprogramming, breath work and several other methods. I was so passionate about the program that I became certified to teach others as a certified healthy lifestyle educator.

I met and taught individuals from all over the world who had come to learn how to heal. I knew I had found a major part of my purpose. It was there that I learned that, oftentimes, "dis-ease" was a manifestation of mental, emotional, and spiritual imbalances. Those imbalances happen because of childhood trauma, unresolved emotional pain, negative thinking, poor lifestyle choices, and not living your soul's purpose.

A year later, I decided to leave the school and resume traveling in my IT job until I could figure out how to create a business doing what I loved. It was at this time that I met a wonderful man.

In the past, every time I broke up with my ex my mother had encouraged me to create a profile on Match, but I was always too scared. One day I thought, what the heck, it's okay to have a pen pal. And a man named Ron messaged me.

We immediately started talking and within a few weeks I was looking forward to reading his messages. He told me he had bought a copy of my book and gave one to his mother and that really touched my heart. A week later he paid for a spa package for me. He asked me on a date for New Year's and we became inseparable after that.

We quickly fell in love, and within the first year I was pregnant and engaged. After having my son, I moved to his hometown. It was extremely difficult as a new mom: not having my mother, not having a support system and having no clue what I was doing. I fell into postpartum depression and the days began to run together. I became resentful of Ron, because I felt like I had to put my dreams on hold while he didn't. Our relationship suffered, and I felt I was getting further and further away from my purpose. I couldn't see a way out.

I prayed to God for help. Ron and I decided to get counseling to learn how we could better support each other, improve our communication and talk about our feelings. It helped us both gain a better perspective on each other's needs and wants. Over time our relationship improved, and I realized that Ron was doing the best he could to support a new family and run his business.

We hired a nanny which gave me more time to focus on taking care of myself. During this time, I started a holistic detox so that I could help myself gain clarity, heal, and improve my wellbeing.

After six weeks I felt renewed, like weight had been lifted and I had so much clarity. Along my journey, I posted content to share what I was doing to help myself. I lost 30 pounds, my skin was glowing, I was back in a size 7, and I felt amazing. Women began to reach out to me for help.

I saw an ad for an eight-week program about how to create your own course and decided to invest in it. Eight weeks later, I opened the door to my first group-coaching program, helping women heal from heartache through holistic detoxing. I enrolled eight women in my first program and it was completely life changing. One participant thanked me for giving her the blueprint to love herself in body, mind, and spirit.

In the program, I take women on a journey towards self-love and healing. I start off by conducting a scan to uncover subconscious beliefs, emotional issues and physical parts of the body that have been impacted due to these low vibrational energies. I then create a customized holistic plan to address the subconscious, emotional, and physical imbalances that are present within.

During our time together, we create a more empowered self-image, release past emotional blockages, eliminate limiting subconscious beliefs, create a healthy lifestyle, and improve the alkalinity of the body through plant-based nutrition. We set goals, create an action plan, and I provide support and accountability to help them stay on course.

Today, I've served over 100 women on their healing journey. I've been featured in magazines, podcasts, television, and national speaking engagements. I will continue to share the power of holistic detoxing to all that I come across because it helped me turn my pain into peace and positioned me to prosper in my purpose.

. . .

Heartache can cause so much pain that we lose a part of ourselves and our purpose. Sometimes we struggle with reclaiming our identity and personal power and it's hard to bounce back. But within you, you have the insurmountable spirit of God that can never be defeated.

No matter where you are right now in your life, know that you have what it takes to rise.

All you have to do is decide, commit to yourself, and take daily action. You are worthy, deserving, gifted, and have a unique purpose to fulfill. Don't let your fears, your past, and painful experiences keep you in bondage.

Know that God has great things in store for you. But you have to be willing to let go of what holds you back, so you can receive an abundant life. You are the only YOU on the planet.

I continue to share my mother's message, "If you get the chance to dance, I hope you dance."

Now go show the world what you're made of!

AISHAH TATUM

Aishah Tatum is the founder of Integrative Wellness and The Fearless Woman Society.

Aishah facilitates extensive coaching programs, workshops and retreats, providing women with the guidance, resources and tools to detox their minds, bodies, and emotions, all so they can manifest their dreams and make permanent changes in their lives.

She also shares some of her deepest, most soul-awakening secrets inside her four books, *Healthy Eating Guide: Eat Clean, Lose Weight & Get Healthy*, *My Vision Journal: A Guided Journal to Assist in the Manifestation of One's Dreams*, *The Fearless Woman: A Book of Affirmations*, and *Girl, Heal: How to Release the Emotional Pain of Your Past, Reclaim Yourself & Get on the Path to Your Purpose*.

As a healthy lifestyle educator, she has participated in the renowned John Maxwell Leadership Trainer program and earned certifications in detox therapy, life, and health coaching. Aishah also holds a masters in business administration and metaphysical sciences, a Bachelor of Science in psychology, and is finishing her Ph.D.

Women who have participated in Aishah's programs applaud her for giving them the "blueprint to living their best lives".

INVITATION FROM THE AUTHOR

If you have a desire to let go of what's holding you back and reclaim your power, I'd like to invite you to watch "Girl, Heal", a powerful training course that walks you through the blueprint for healing past emotional pain, becoming fearlessly confident, and living on purpose.

https://www.detoxyouremotions.com/GirlHealprivatetraining

CONNECT WITH THE AUTHOR

Business Name: Integrative Wellness
Website: www.aishahtatum.com
Facebook: www.facebook.com/AishahTatum
Email: aishah@aishahtatum.com

Decide how old you want to live. Subtract the number of years you are now. That is the number of years you still have to live your best life! It is never too late to start again.

Sharon Muscet

There is nothing like a near-death experience to lead you to reevaluate your life. Thanks to two brushes with death I know just how lucky I am to be here, and I definitely do not sweat the small stuff anymore. When you look death in the eyes, all the things we usually stress about are no longer important.

I am the first to admit I was living a blessed life. It was in 2004, at the height of my corporate career as a PR and marketing executive in London, travelling the world with a global wine company that I had a *freak* accident. This accident was to change my life forever.

I was on a work trip in my hometown of Adelaide. We had brought twenty of our top distributors from around the world to Australia for a two-week trip, with our first stop being our winery and then on to Adelaide's beautiful beaches.

On the first day of the trip I decided to go for a paddle in the water at a popular beach. I was being a bit silly, walking in the water until I was knee-deep and kicking my legs around. The water was murky, and I took a step and saw a stingray hidden in the sandy seabed. I scared it as much as it scared me, and as a defense mechanism it flicked its tail up.

I stepped straight on the stingray's tail and was struck at the bottom of my left foot just under my third and fourth toes. It was bleeding, and I felt like I had been stabbed with a razor-sharp needle.

Cast your mind back to Steve Irwin, the famous Australian Crocodile Hunter. He had an encounter with a stingray where the barb from its tail went through his heart and cost him his life. His accident happened two years after mine.

My injury was painful, but I just patched it up and pushed on. At this stage in my international career, I was regularly working seventy hours a week and I was a self-described "workaholic". I was single, living the high life, had set myself up very well financially, and was literally married to my job.

The next morning I woke up feeling unwell, so I went to the doctor for antibiotics and they told me to stay off my feet, but I couldn't. I battled on for the next week. At the end of the trip I flew back to London and by the time the plane landed my foot had blown up like a balloon.

By this time, I had developed a chronic infection. The stingray barb has serrated edges and a sharp point. The underside produces a venom which can be fatal to humans. I had an infection setting in and, unbeknownst to me, there was also extensive nerve damage to my foot.

Despite seeking urgent treatment in London including strong antibiotics and three surgeries, the infection became worse. After three months in hospital, I was told the only option may be to amputate my toes or foot.

That's when my employer stepped in. They flew me back to my hometown of Adelaide so I could go to the Royal Adelaide Hospital. They had just opened a foot clinic and there was a team of eight doctors waiting for me. They told me straight up that I was facing at least another eighteen months off my feet and that I could still lose my toes or foot, or even die.

The result of the stingray barb was horrendous. I spent a total of two years in and out of hospital, in a wheelchair and with a PICC line attached to my arm. I had a total of ten operations, and on two occasions was fighting to save my left foot from amputation. The toxins that ravaged through my body played havoc with me, as did the antibiotics permanently pumped through me. My liver was badly affected and, for a time, the whites of my eyes turned orange.

I was in despair; I had been forced to return to Australia to convalesce with family and friends. The house I owned was being rented out, so I was homeless and living on friends' couches in between hospital stays. After twelve months, I had to make the difficult decision to relinquish my role with the company. I was left with a permanent partial disability of my left foot. My foot now has plates and screws inserted and I have peripheral neuropathy, meaning I have lost feeling in my left foot.

These were some of the toughest days of my life, and to make matters worse I nearly lost my life on two occasions. It was during surgery number five that I looked death straight in the eye. I developed a blood clot to my lungs following a surgery on my foot and leg. The doctors believe it broke away from my foot and travelled up my body. It nearly killed me. That was the point when I started to give up. Up until then I had remained positive, but now I was fighting for my life. I had pain in my chest like I have never experienced before. The doctor told me to prepare myself, I may die from this. I was scared. But I remember completely surrendering to the situation. I said to myself, I am done with fighting this. I give up all control now. If I am meant to have my foot amputated, or if I am meant to die, then so be it.

The moment I surrendered, my foot and my body started to heal.

Until this time I had been alone for most of my treatment in Adelaide as my family lived hours away. Then I reconnected with an old friend who stepped in to support me during my darkest hours. This friend would go on to become my husband and father of my two children— Luka and Hugo.

Things were looking up. I had survived this horrendous ordeal and was able to keep my foot. However, some years after my tenth surgery, another tragedy hit when I had a heart attack. I stared death in the face again. I fought for my life. I wasn't ready to go. I remember thinking at the time, I have my boys now. I still have so much life to live. And I fought the biggest fight of my life that day.

About one week after this happened, I was travelling with my husband and the boys to the playground. Feeling too weak to get out of the car I sat inside and watched them play, when this overwhelming sense of peace came over me. I had an epiphany. I thought, I have survived two brushes with death. If I was meant to be gone, I'd be gone but I'm here, and I am here for a reason.

Something happened inside me that day; I no longer feared anything, including death. A light came on inside me and I felt fearless, like I could achieve anything. Upon reflection, I can now say that the accident was the best thing that ever happened to me.

Two years is a very long time to be off your feet, but I decided to devote myself to the things I had always wanted to do. There is something happening here, I thought to myself, I am being prepared for something bigger and better than I have ever thought possible. I believed that. I had to. There was no other option. I refused to play the victim.

I knew I had to keep my spirits up, to stay as positive as I could during one of the most difficult times of my life. First, I took up singing lessons. Singing made me so happy and I looked forward to it every week. It made my heart sing. I took up knitting as I had always wanted to knit myself a scarf. I found this incredibly meditative. I took up mosaic classes and immersed myself in the creative process of mosaics and made many things for myself. I studied to become a marriage celebrant—something I had always wanted to do. I delved further into meditation and began teaching meditation classes to others. I learned about numerology and began to complete numerology charts for people. I became qualified at Reiki and energy healing. I opened a healing practice and had weekly clients who would come to see me.

What began to happen was very interesting—*through being of service to other people and helping others, it was aiding in my own healing.*

Despite my challenges with my physical health and ongoing operations on my foot (my healing took six years in total), I was in a very good place spiritually, emotionally, and mentally. I was a mom now. Something I never thought I would be. I was so happy. They were my little miracles. With them, my life took on a whole new meaning.

Once the boys were two years and three years old and my health was back on track, I started up a network marketing business with a worldwide company. My accident had set me back hundreds and thousands of dollars in lost earnings. So, I got to work, not only for me but for my husband and children as well. And remember, a light had now come on inside me and I felt fearless, that I could achieve anything.

Little did I know that that light and fearlessness meant that within eighteen months I would achieve international success and recognition with the company and go on to receive a global award in front of 15,000 other consultants.

I had grown my business to the position of vice president very quickly and had been invited to travel to Las Vegas for the company's annual conference. I was told prior to their awards evening that I was one of the top five consultants in the company (out of their 250,000 consultants) in the running for their Global Organizational Sponsoring Award. This meant that in the last year I had introduced more people into the business than anyone else. I couldn't believe it!

It was the night of the awards. I was dressed in a black and silver evening gown, with the highest of heels. I had my hair and makeup done for the occasion and I felt so beautiful. There I was, up on stage in front of 15,000 people. It was like the Oscars; there were lights, cameras, people cheering. I'd never been to anything like it. I came out on stage as one of the top five consultants, and got the surprise of my life when my name was announced as their *Number 1 Consultant in the World for Organizational Sponsoring*! It was totally unexpected, and a career highlight for me. It confirmed for me what I could do if my belief system was strong.

I once heard someone say that what happens to you in life is no accident. Each little experience is like a jigsaw piece. You piece it all together, bit by bit, to create something extraordinary. That is what I believe happened to me. Piece by piece, like a jigsaw, it was all coming together. Every little experience was building upon the next and the next, to create a life that was truly magical. Despite the obstacles, I continued to believe there was something incredible awaiting me. I wasn't sure what, but I had faith.

And then, just as everything was going well for me, tragedy struck again. My marriage suddenly ended. There had been betrayal involved, and my heart was well and truly broken. I was forced from my home with my two children. For the next two years I fought for what was rightfully mine. After a long battle with lawyers it wasn't to be, and I was left with nothing. Everything I had built up from my corporate career, gone. The loss of my marriage, the betrayal and financial abuse, and the battle with lawyers knocked the wind from my sails. Everything I had worked for and owned, up until this point, was gone. It took every ounce of my strength to get up in the mornings to be there for my children. They were what kept me going.

This had an impact on my network marketing business, and within a year that was gone as well. Friends and business partners had betrayed me, and now I had lost it all. I don't know how I got through those days. I had suffered so much loss, and I didn't know how much more I could take. Putting one foot in front of the other was all I could do. I didn't know where life would lead me. That light that had once come on inside me, and that fearlessness, was now gone. Instead of light, I saw darkness, and instead of living fearlessly, I now lived in fear of my future for not only myself but my children as well.

Around this time my best friend's father passed away. Given I was a marriage celebrant, she asked me to conduct his entire funeral service, to be his funeral celebrant. A funeral celebrant comes into people's lives when they are sad and grieving for the loss of someone they love. They write and lead the entire funeral service. I had conducted several weddings ceremonies, but I had never conducted a funeral before.

I was nervous when my friend asked me. To be honest, I didn't know how I would feel leading a funeral. Would I be ok? How would I cope? How would I feel seeing my friend and others sad and crying? Would I cry myself, during the service? All these thoughts made me uncomfortable. After some time reflecting however, I realized I was making it all about me, and it was not about me at all. This was for my friend, her family, and her father. I was there to be of service. So, I said yes, and I conducted the funeral service for my friend's father.

Being able to be there for all of them at one of the saddest times in their lives and deliver a beautiful service that they would remember was so rewarding for me. I recall driving home to my empty house thinking, it just feels right, I cannot describe it, but I know I am where I am meant to be. It was the moment I realized I had just *lived on purpose*. I have been living on purpose ever since.

Since then I have conducted several hundred celebrations of life for those who have passed, ranging from a baby at sixteen weeks gestation, right up until the age of 106 years old. All celebrations are unique. It is the most rewarding work. Everything that had happened up until this point had led me to this path.

There were days when I didn't want to get out of bed, given the sadness going on in my day-to-day life. But then I would receive a phone call from a funeral home, saying a family had just lost their child. And suddenly, it wasn't about me anymore, and I had to be there one hundred percent for that family. It reconfirmed the lesson I had learned in earlier years—*through being of service to other people and helping others, it was aiding in my own healing.*

During the period of COVID19, I worked with many families who lost a loved one to suicide. The work I do comes from a place in my heart, of deep love and connection. In my experiences of working with these families and hearing their loved one's life stories, I discovered that every single life has a meaning and a purpose. We all have an incredible story to share. We all have life lessons within us that we can share with others. This work also reinforced just how fragile life really is—that we need to live each day like it is our last, and live it fearlessly and shine our light so bright.

Through this work I made another discovery, and this discovery was the most incredible of them all. There is a famous quote by the late Dr. Wayne Dyer which says, "When we change the way we look at things, the things we look at change."

Through my work, I discovered this . . .

Death is LOVE.

I see love in its finest form. I do not work in the death industry; I am in the industry of love.

As I sit with a family, I hear their most personal feelings about love when their loved one passes. I hear the most incredible love stories. I see the love a parent has for their child and a child has for their parent. I hear stories of dysfunction, people torn apart by love. I see hearts breaking in front of me every day, but it's born out of love. I hear and see the absolute devastation at the loss of life. This devastation and this grief are all born out of love.

Each day, I witness love in its purest form. We are all born into love and we all leave this world in love. As Deepak Chopra says, "Love is the most powerful force in the Universe." I wholeheartedly agree.

I have gone on to become one of Australia's foremost experts in healing and loss. I am now an international speaker, published author, award-winning thought leader, and founder of *The Love in Death* movement.

With my light shining bright, and my fearlessness returned, I set myself another goal to transform the lives of the living. In November 2019, I published my first book, *7 Life Lessons Learned Through Loss: Powerful Stories of Love, Hope, Transformation and Legacy*. This book shares powerful stories, life lessons and love stories from those who have passed with a view to helping others live their best life.

Life for me is one continuous journey. I show my boys how to live a life in service to others. I show them to never take a day for granted. I show them that they are capable of overcoming any obstacle. I am someone who has rebuilt her life and career so many times, each time believing it is for something better. I am a true believer that life happens *for* you, not *to* you. Every setback in our life, allows for an even greater comeback.

In early 2020, I was forced to have my eleventh surgery on my foot—yes trouble from my accident arose again! However, I used the three months of recovery to embark upon another self-discovery journey.

I commenced studying with world-renowned therapist Marisa Peer, and I am so proud to be one of the first *Licensed Rapid Transformational Practitioners* in Australia. Once again, I was being led to live a life of service in the healing of others. I help set people free from their limiting beliefs, from what is holding them back, so they can be free to live the life they are destined to live. To turn on their own light within, so they can live fearlessly. This is just another step forward in my remarkable journey.

Some people become a victim to life's adversities; others find meaning and purpose in their life and use it for the good of others. The latter was the case for me. I found meaning in my life through all of my adversities. I discovered my life's purpose.

Gandhi said, "In a gentle way, we can shake the world." I believe that in a gentle way we can all do just that. Every single life has a meaning and a purpose. We are all here to make an impact in this world. Even by making an impact in one person's life, you have been of service to humanity. All it takes is that light within you, and that fearlessness to make it happen.

If there is one thing I have learned, it is that the only thing we can control in our life is our mind. We cannot control the actions of others, what will happen from one day to the next, or when we will die. All we can control is how we choose to respond to the events that happen in our lives.

Decide how old you want to live. Subtract the number of years you are now. That is the number of years you have to live your best life! It is never too late to start again. It is never too late to switch that light on and live it fearlessly.

My dream is to live to 100 years old. I am forty-nine years young, so I have fifty-one years to live my best life. I am not even halfway there yet. I am only just getting started!

SHARON MUSCET

Sharon Muscet is one of Australia's foremost experts on healing and loss.

As a highly sought-after funeral celebrant, Sharon has worked with thousands of individuals experiencing the realities of death, giving her privileged insight into how to cope with grief and loss.

Sharon is an international speaker, an award-winning thought leader, the founder of *The Love in Death* movement. She is also a published author, and in her book, *7 Life Lessons Learned Through Loss*, Sharon shares powerful stories of love, hope, transformation, and legacy.

Sharon is a licensed rapid transformational practitioner, having trained with world-renowned therapist Marisa Peer. Sharon's therapy work achieves rapid and powerful results for a range of issues, working with both children and adults around the world. She lives her life in service of healing others.

Sharon resides in Australia and is the proud mother of two boys.

INVITATION FROM THE AUTHOR

Do you feel that there is something holding you back from reaching your full potential? Perhaps you have tried therapy before but nothing seems to work. Rapid Transformational Therapy (RTT) is different— we go deeper. We go to the root cause and heal it.

If you have had setbacks, have limiting beliefs, or you feel something is holding you back, contact me for a FREE strategy call:

https://calendly.com/sharonmuscet

As a *RTT Practitioner, I* will help you to identify your barriers, break through your negative patterns and heal your emotional wounds, so you can truly thrive!

CONNECT WITH THE AUTHOR

Business Name: Sharon Muscet
Website: www.sharonmuscet.com
Facebook: www.facebook.com/sharon.muscet/
Email: connect@sharonmuscet.com

———

Be unapologetically you, unafraid to set the world on fire, living your life of passion and purpose.

Johanna Clark

I was just a regular seventeen-year-old girl. Finishing off year eleven, studying hard to get good marks, and preparing for exams. I was doing all the right things. Choosing subjects that I didn't enjoy, like maths methods, over ones I loved and was passionate about, like decorative metalwork and jewelry making. The tougher subjects would ensure I got the ENTER score I needed to get into university. Or so they said. And I wholeheartedly believed what society and my teachers were pushing me towards. Get good grades, get into university, graduate, and build a career. It was the only option, and I would be a massive failure if I chose another path. When I wasn't studying or spending time with my boyfriend, I was scrapbooking, jewelry making, lead lighting. You name it, I was trying it.

Just a regular seventeen-year-old girl. Until I wasn't. It was a Sunday. After dance rehearsals I met up with my boyfriend for lunch. Steven and I had been together for three years and I was completely head over heels in love with him. It was young love, a tumultuous relationship, but I was his and that was all I wanted. He left our lunch to go for a motorbike ride with his mates. That was the last time I ever saw him alive. He had just turned eighteen, and he didn't wait one minute before getting his road bike license and a brand-new shiny Yamaha road bike. I remember walking home to my Nan's house and hearing the ambulances. I thought to myself, you know what, that could be Steven. But I banished the thought.

When I walked in the door I got a phone call from one of his friends. Steven had had an accident and I needed to come right away. I had no idea that my life was about to change forever. In the car ride there I rang his friend again to ask for an update. He told me that Steven was dead. I can still take myself right back to that moment. I can still feel how I felt—like my heart fell out of my chest and onto the car floor. I remember running down the street towards the accident, screaming. The next few days were a blur. I begged aloud for a sign that he was still around me, and I wished desperately to join him if he was.

By the time year twelve started I had pulled myself together enough to go through the paces. Attending school, doing the subjects I hated, studying, working, and a whole lot of partying. I tried to fill the void that Steven had left behind in the worst kinds of ways. But I was lucky. I had an amazing group of girlfriends and family to help me through with no judgments, just love and caring.

As I was getting close to graduating, I met a man named Joel. He was cheeky, a little bit naughty. Just my type. We hit it off. One night I shared my story with him and he told me how his brother had also passed away in a road bike accident. He told me that I would never get over losing Steven, but that I needed to learn to live without him. He showed me that life was a gift, a blessing, and I decided that if Steven couldn't live his then I damn well wasn't going to waste mine. Steven's passing gave me the gift of living my life with no regrets. As hard as it is to say that his passing gave me a gift, I needed to give it a positive meaning so I could move on, and honoring his life by truly living mine was the best I could do.

Joel moved down to Warrnambool to live with me. I graduated high school, started a bachelor's degree of Nursing/Midwifery and started on my path to a normal life. Then I fell pregnant with our first child. I was eighteen, a university student, and working three jobs. As overwhelming as it was, I could not have been happier. All I had ever wanted to be was a mother. I was always obsessed with babies and could not wait for the day I had my own. I copped a fair bit of flack when we announced it. I had ruined my life. I had so much potential and now it was wasted. I would never become anything. I was a failure. Most of these comments came from people whose opinion should not have mattered to me. They didn't know me. And as well-meaning as some of them may have been, the comments ran deep. I let their words define me for far too long. But they also gave me the unexpected gift of a desire to prove them all wrong. I deferred from my studies, got a full-time job, and worked up until I gave birth to my first son, Ezekiel.

My goodness did I love being his mother. I held him twenty-four seven. I doted on him, I never let anyone else hold or care for him. But I also felt lost and alone. I felt like I didn't have a purpose, like I had nothing to look forward to and nothing to keep my brain busy. I believed that I was a terrible mother. Why couldn't I be happy being at home and caring for my baby? Why wasn't that enough for me? I felt every prick of guilt. But as I had vowed to live life to the fullest, I decided to get to work. I walked down to the local TAFE, baby in tow, and enrolled in a bookkeeping course and got started right away. I also taught myself how to sew to earn some money and keep my mind busy and positive in the quiet moments at home.

It was a juggle, but I managed to do it all. I started an online business and sold my wares at a market with a friend. All whilst studying and progressing to a Diploma of Accounting. After I had my second son, Nathaniel, I decided to go back to university to become an accountant.

I was twenty-one, which meant that I was now a mature age student and that my ENTER score which I'd worked so hard for was no longer valid. But since I had completed the Diploma in Accounting I was able to use it as my entry into the degree.

Nathaniel was six months old when I started the diploma. On my first day, I got in trouble for having my phone on. And when I came home that night I fainted from mastitis. I hadn't gone that long without breastfeeding before and it knocked me for six. I contemplated never going back. But that little voice in the back of my head wouldn't let me give up or give in. To make things a little crazier, I had my third baby boy, Milo, during my second year. I finished that degree in three years, graduating with a distinction average, and pregnant with my fourth child. This made it impossible to get a job after I graduated, so all that work, I believed, had been for nothing. I had pushed and pushed myself—running my sewing business, Joeyjellybean, whilst studying, parenting, and trying to keep my relationship together—for nothing.

Still, I threw myself into my business. A new baby brings change and upheaval with them; and when my fourth child was born, my daughter, Esmae, the gears began to turn for my business, too. I dragged my husband down to Melbourne for two days, with a newborn, to attend a screen printing class. Fabrics and patterns were the star of my sewing business. I loved finding unique fabrics to create with. But deep down I wanted the freedom to design my own patterns. I remember sitting up late in the hotel room after the class with a thumping migraine, my brain in a buzz with ideas, possibilities, and a new sense of purpose. I was getting close to what I was meant to do. It was the first time I had allowed myself to believe that a path of self-employment—in a career where I didn't hold a piece of paper giving me permission—was possible.

I had found my niche. I was unapologetically standing out from the crowd and showing my true creative side. It was quirky, weird, and fun!

Time became my biggest problem. I had none. With four kids and a booming business I decided the next step was to manufacture my baby clothing overseas. I thought this would solve my problem—get me off the tools so I could work on the business not in it. I took my four children with me to the bank and got myself a personal loan. This paid for my first drop and gave me the confidence boost I needed to take the next step. The bank thought I could do it. It couldn't be that hard, right? Well, if there was a mistake to be made, I damn well made it. Faults in manufacturing, label issues, freight, import tax, GST, exchange rate differences, and the difficulties of wholesale. I thought, if you build it, they will come. No! That wasn't the case.

When I fell pregnant with my fifth child I decided enough was enough. I couldn't handle the stress anymore, and I wanted to enjoy my children. I stopped manufacturing, which left me with a massive debt and a shed full of stock. I still needed to work, but I chose, for the sake of my baby boy, August, to slow it down a bit, and went back to screen printing and sewing baby bibs. I came up with a collection of Australian designs and launched them to the market. They went gangbusters.

But I still had huge limiting beliefs around how I handled business and money, beliefs that held me back from truly succeeding for longer than I would like to admit. With five children, I was now busier than ever. Around this time, I decided to teach myself graphic design, so I could design patterns and have them digitally printed onto the fabric. I did an online course on Adobe Illustrator and once again felt that overwhelming sense of purpose. THIS was what I was meant to be doing. This made my heart sing. I could lose hours in it. It made my brain explode with possibilities and endless opportunities.

Then my husband purchased a large format printer and decided to open a sign writing business. He was lacking in design skills so I took on that role too, and we started the business together. A few months later, the building next to ours became available and we made the split second decision to open a clothing boutique. I could manage both as I was always on site, and Joel could come and go as needed, as he was mostly out doing quotes, installations, or working his other contract as a Postie.

This was when I experienced my first real burnout. I thought I could juggle full-time work, looking after the house, my children, and running Joeyjellybean at night. I thought my body didn't have a limit; I could push it and push it and it would never let me down. First it started with an eye twitch that wouldn't go away. Then my speech started to slur, my brain was foggy, and I experienced some scary memory loss. The last straw was when my joints were so painful I could hardly lift my children up. I finally took myself to the doctor, thinking something was seriously wrong with me. I was dying, or so Dr. Google told me. My doctor asked me lots of questions, ran the routine checks, then asked me about my life and lifestyle. I will never forget his face when I reeled off everything I did daily, my responsibilities, and all my stresses. He looked at me quite sternly and said, "Johanna, you are severely burnt out. If you don't stop right now I will have to admit you to hospital and force you to rest."

I knew what I had to do, but I didn't want to. I had to give up Joeyjellybean. It was my baby. It had saved me from falling into a deep depression, gave me a sense of purpose, my own money, and not to mention the joy I felt being creative. But I made the decision to close it down. I can't describe the relief I felt when I finally made that decision and announced its closure. I realized right away I was holding onto it for all the wrong reasons. Closing that chapter of my life was the right decision, and gave me the time and direction to start my business, Pink Nade, a statement earring brand.

I had just started wearing earrings again after having children (the ear ripping phase was REAL fun). Now that I was working full-time, I could wear them again. The confidence that I felt wearing a killer pair of statement earrings and a bangin' lippy was like no other, and I wanted to share that with other women. And it made sense for the store as I could design and create them to compliment the clothing range. I already had the skills I needed to start designing. I found a laser cutting business, researched supplies, spent hours trialing and testing until I was happy with what I had produced. I felt my way through the entire process and began to trust my gut. I wore that first pair of earrings with pride.

Around this time, a friend of mine had just returned from a seminar with Tony Robbins. He was radiating positive energy and I wanted what he had. So I decided to invest in myself and purchased a ticket, a VIP ticket, just to show myself I truly believed I was worth it. A few of my friends also decided to attend and we all made the flight to Sydney together.

My burnout had returned, and this time my symptoms were more severe. On the first morning of the seminar I was shaking with fear. But I had this feeling in my gut that I could change this—that if I went all in at the seminar I could banish my burnouts and get back to living a normal life.

8000 men and women all together in one room, facing their fears and playing like children. We danced, screamed, hugged, and sweated.

Then, they asked us to walk on fire. I couldn't do it. My stomach felt like a washing machine as I walked outside towards the burning hot coals lined up along the ground. I watched as, one by one, each person in front of me stormed across the crackling coals, proving to themselves they were capable of anything they put their minds to.

It was my turn. I felt a flicker of hesitancy. Then something in my mind just switched. I CAN DO THIS! I can't remember walking on the coals, only coming out the other side with the greatest sense of pride, achievement, and love for myself. We screamed in celebration like we never had before. It was electrifying. What a high! I finally BELIEVED I could succeed. That I was enough, smart enough, capable enough, and deserving of everything I ever dreamed.

I wasn't going to let anything stop me this time. We went from turning over $2000 a month in my earring business to $20,000 straight away. Nothing had changed, just my mindset and my belief that I could do it. I was determined and unstoppable. I hired two mentors. As Tony Robbins says, "Don't reinvent the wheel, learn from someone who has already been there and done it." This was the best business decision I have ever made.

I truly believe in the power of the universe—that there is 'something' out there, guiding us along a path, rooting for us to follow our passions and live a fulfilling life. I also believe there is something inside everyone—a hidden gem desperate to be uncovered, to be given the light to truly shine. I feel that I have been peeling back the layers, that my life so far has been chipping away at that little gem inside of myself. Now the light is starting to shine through and I am living my life with more passion and purpose every day. The universe has thrown her fair share of challenges my way, but I know she is just testing me to see if I am really listening.

I am now running three six-figure businesses with HUGE goals for the future and a fire in my belly to succeed at all costs. I have a team of incredible women working alongside me. I have two amazing mentors and have become a mentor myself, and feel incredibly fulfilled being able to support other women in their business journey. Not only with the skills needed to succeed, but also helping them embrace their power, to help them see that they are worthy and that they are enough, and that they deserve to achieve their greatest dreams. I recently opened a dedicated retail store for Pink Nade, and I am putting this out to the universe right now: you WILL see Pink Nade stores in shopping centers around Australia in the future.

What you think, you can become.

JOHANNA CLARK

Johanna Clark discovered her passion in life when she founded her own jewellery line, Pink Nade, and has gone on to open a ladies fashion store, Pink Nade Boutique, which she runs with a team of incredible women by her side. Crafty at heart, she also helps her husband run a sign writing business called Loud Signs from their home in rural Victoria.

Johanna is a mother of five beautiful children. She has always dreamed of becoming a mother and having a flexible, fulfilling career where she can be there for her children, but also achieve her big, lofty goals and live a life of purpose.

She is a massive supporter of women supporting women. She began Pink Nade in the hopes of helping women find their power, to truly believe in themselves, and to live life to the fullest and with colour and passion.

Johanna herself lives a life of no regrets and no longer lets fear hold her back from following her passion and dreams. She has a kind heart, and LOVES to dance. She values self education and personal development, believing that to live is to grow.

INVITATION FROM THE AUTHOR

Ready to set the world on fire? Visit our website and shop our range of statement accessories. We also have a Girl Gang if you're looking for a community of women who will support and lift you up. Can't wait to see you rise!

CONNECT WITH THE AUTHOR

Business name: Pink Nade
Website: www.pinknade.com.au
Facebook: www.facebook.com/pinknade
Email: johanna@pinknade.com.au

Do hard things: Let your frustrations fuel your future.

Ashley Dwyer

We all have an idea of what life will be like when we finally grow up. For me, I thought I would go away to college, graduate from pharmacy school, meet the man of my dreams, fall madly in love and have children together. We would then live happily ever after. Little did I know how differently life would turn out.

My parents certainly didn't live the fairy tale of my dreams. Perhaps that was why I desired it so badly for myself. My parents divorced when I was fourteen and my dad moved out. I would live with my mother on the weekdays and my father on the weekends. Shortly after their divorce, we found out that my grandmother, my dad's mother, had stage four breast cancer. She had always been my rock and she inspired me with her amazing stories. Every weekend I would sit with her and listen as she told me about her life. A part of me died with her as I watched her shrivel away and finally pass on.

At nineteen, my mother and I moved over six hours away from my friends, family, and the place I had called home my entire life, and I began work at a pharmacy. No one knew me, and I could finally have a fresh start. The beaches were beautiful. I enrolled in college and my only goal was to read as many books as possible from my towel on the beach and to learn how to surf. That's when he entered the picture.

He was one of those cool guys. He surfed every day before and after work, and he was alluring in a mysterious way. He said he would teach me to surf and invited me out after work. I barely knew him. I just knew I wanted to surf, and he knew how. That was all I cared about.

Tension at home had been brewing. My mother was fiercely depressed. Her anger over my brothers choosing to remain with my dad instead of her would bubble over and she would lash out at the nearest person. One night it got so bad that I decided to stay over at a friend's house. She told me not to come home at all. The next day she showed up at my workplace and removed the plates from my car. That was the day that I realized I was homeless, in a new town and a new place where I barely knew anyone. I had the clothes on my back and nothing more. One of my coworkers allowed me to sleep on her couch in exchange for babysitting. This was the first time in my life I knew hunger.

One day my surfing buddy told me that he had an extra room at his place and I was welcome to stay there. He said he had a bed that I could sleep in. I didn't know he meant his bed.

It turned out my new surfing buddy was in recovery from drug and alcohol addiction. At first it was all fun and games. We would get up every morning at 5 a.m. and ride our bikes to the McDonalds before heading to the beach. We would surf till the afternoon and come in to nap and shower. Then it was back to the beach to meet the waves.

He started drinking. I lied to my friends and coworkers about the bruises that now covered my body. I blamed surfing and biking. I knew perfectly well how to get out of the way of the sharp fin attached to my board. And it didn't leave large bruises on my arms that resembled hand prints. Was this abuse? I asked myself. He said he loved me.

One night he forced himself on me and flushed my birth control pills down the toilet. A month later I found out I was pregnant. I was a mixture of excited and terrified all at once. Surely this would make him stop drinking and stop hurting me. My parents would be furious and ashamed, and sure enough, when I told them, they were livid.

We had just found out that we were having a boy. He called his sister excitedly to tell her, and she asked if he was sure it was his. He began to drink again. He got violent. He grabbed my hair and beat my head against the wall and the counter. I screamed for help hoping the neighbors would hear. I tried to call the police, but he grabbed my hand that was holding the phone, breaking my fingers. Clutching my left hand, I rushed to pack my things into my little red Honda Civic. I couldn't find my shoes. He had taken them. It was raining outside, and I ran to my car barefoot, the mud squishing between my toes. He followed behind, tried to apologize. But I got in the car and drove away.

I was alone with nowhere to go. Pregnant. With broken fingers. No shoes. Muddy feet. Unsure of what to do next. My hand throbbed. The pain radiated up my arm to my shoulder and my neck. My fingers were as broken as my heart was. I drove to the hospital. I had nowhere else to go. I was twenty and once again homeless.

A friend called my mother and convinced her to let me come back home. No one would hire me in my pregnant state. But I had a good guy friend. We would cook dinner together and just hang out. He was my escape. He was protective of me and so incredibly understanding. Then I had my son.

My friend came to the hospital to see us both. We had just found out that my son was deaf. They ran the newborn hearing screen for hours and hours. Was this my fault? I assumed it had to be something I did while I was pregnant.

After my son was born, my friend slowly disappeared from my life. In other words, he ghosted me. One night, while my son was with my mother, I ran into his dad. He grabbed me before I could walk away, so I punched him in the face. He called the cops. I drove to the pier and took 57 Percocets before driving to my friend's place. He had another girl in his apartment. When I told him what I had done, he drove me to the ER and dropped me off. I just wanted to die. I couldn't live like this anymore. No one wanted me. My past trauma, the postpartum depression, my hormones and the sleep depression were overwhelming me.

As my liver began to fail they tried to give me charcoal. I vomited black chunks of what they were forcing down my throat onto the green hospital curtains. I prayed to God to forgive me for what I had done as I felt myself float in and out of consciousness. I needed to be transported to another hospital so they loaded me into the ambulance and on the way I passed out.

When I awoke, I was in a strange new place. I was in critical care and I would be lucky to live three days, they told me. I was dying. Sometime that night DSS showed up. My mother had called. She had my son with her. The next day my dad and his new wife came to say goodbye. No one else bothered. No one else cared enough. I spent the next two weeks in and out of consciousness. Then I woke up.

"It looks like you are going to pull through," the travel nurse told me, and he squeezed my hand as tears rolled down my face. He told me it was okay, that I just had postpartum depression, that this happened to women all the time.

A week later they discharged me, and I went home to my mother's house. I wasn't allowed to leave the house and I was watched like a hawk. I had no freedom. I couldn't go to the toilet, or shower with the bathroom door closed. My caseworker from DSS came for regular visits. This wasn't a bad thing. My mother told me not to talk to Susan, but I told her everything. I told her everything because I was scared. Scared of what was going to happen to me. Scared of what was going to happen to my baby. Scared for my life. She helped me get a domestic violence protection order and assured me that my son would never end up with his dad.

My guy friend came around for the first time since dropping me off at the hospital. Things were normal between us. He was my best friend again. Most evenings he would make me dinner and we would sit on his couch and watch TV. Every night I would fall asleep beside him. He would feed my son and change his diaper for me. Sometimes he would fall asleep with me. One night, he kissed me.

I met Susan for lunch one day. She said she had talked to my mother and she felt I wasn't being honest about how things were going at home. She arranged for me to stay with a friend in a spare bedroom while I started a new job. Two months later she helped me get my very first condo. My guy friend and I started dating and things were beginning to look up.

When my son was three years old, Tim asked me to marry him and a little over a month later, we were married. I thought my life would finally be complete. I had it all. A loving husband, my own little family, and even a stepson who I loved and adored.

Then, in November 2013 the pharmacy I worked at was robbed. The thief held a gun to my back until I gave him the drugs that he demanded. No one was hurt, but a few days later the owner announced he would close our store, claiming he couldn't keep us safe anymore. I was dumbfounded. What would I do now? I had a family to care for.

In the weeks following, my husband would accuse me of being lazy, as I was still unemployed. I had just lost a job I thought I loved. I was having nightmares and flashbacks about the robbery—the feeling of the gun pressed into my spine, my coworkers kicked to the floor, their hands bound in zip ties. I finally found another pharmacy job.

Then my husband decided that we should move away, six hours west, closer to my old home. He suggested that it would be easier for me and Skyler with my dad close by. Little did I know he was moving us there to leave us. He encouraged me to go back to school to study massage therapy as it was something I had always wanted to do.

I started school on Monday, and on Friday I came home to an empty house. Tim had left and taken everything with him. When Thanksgiving came and went I knew he wasn't coming home. My son stayed with my parents so that I could finish school. I was so hurt inside. I couldn't handle the pain, so I tried to block it out in any way possible. I went out with a different guy nearly every night to numb my own self-hatred and pain. I allowed my lack of confidence and self-esteem to control me for too long.

Finally, I graduated from massage school. I passed my national exam and got my license in hand. It was time to go to work.

My first paycheck as an independent contractor was for $31. $31 and $950 in rent, childcare, electricity, and water to pay. I worked for two weeks for that $31. Discouraged didn't even describe the way I felt at the time.

But I focused on making sure my clients saw the value in coming back to see me for continued services. I made sure that they knew my hours and schedule. It worked, and I started to get busier.

I began to offer massages for people at their home. One day a woman called me out of the blue and offered me a space to rent in her yoga studio. $150 per month. I wanted to jump on it, but I was scared because I hadn't even thought about working for myself.

I finally decided to take the leap and go for it. I would just need three or four clients a month. What would it hurt to try? How badly could I lose?

I moved in right after Christmas. Her studio was a beautiful jewel toned crayon box. It was so serene, nestled in the center of a larger building of renovated lofts.

I was excited, yet clueless. I made lots of beginner's mistakes, but I was seeing far more clients in my office than at my regular forty-hour-a-week massage job. I was finally making money doing what I loved. Then the business next door started teaching drum lessons. Yes. Drum lessons. Next to a massage and yoga studio.

After many days of trying to work around the drum teacher's schedule, I went to my landlord and asked for help with the noise. She led me to a room that had last been used as a recording studio. She went on to tell me that they had been evicted the past week for not being able to pay their rent, and to top it all off, it was sound insulated. For $75 more I could move into a space of my very own. So, I took the plunge.

Four months later, I left my full-time job to work for myself. I was busier than I had been in months. I was a real self-employed business owner now and it was amazing. It also came with a learning curve— networking, marketing, money management—so many new things. I read business books, I watched YouTube videos. I couldn't get enough.

My practice grew, and I moved into another office and opened a second single office location to accommodate my growth. This would be my first attempt at managing people. I started them off as independent contractors like many in my industry, but time revealed the flaws in the model. When I announced in October that on January 1 I would make them employees, they all quit. So, I hired more massage therapists. We were growing and excelling.

I started writing education courses, and soon the Massage Innovation Network for Therapists was born. The Network grew and as it grew, I began to realize that I had a gift in teaching, coaching, and consulting. My business had been through a lot and I had personally been through a lot. It had prepared me to help others in a way that I never imagined.

In the fall of 2020, I went back to school to get certified as a coach and consultant so that I could better help my students run their businesses and help them get through their own hardships. I felt as if I was on top of the world. I was one of the only coaches and consultants in my industry with training of any kind.

In January 2020, I signed the contract to write my first book. I was excited, but completely unprepared for what was to come. I spent six weeks writing to meet my March 16 deadline.

At this point, the coronavirus was all anyone was talking about. When the state shut down we were in disbelief. But two weeks was doable. We could survive the fortnight. Then we hit the two-month mark. I began to question it all. How would we get through this? I thought we would be ruined.

I began to hustle my homemade soy candles that I had sold in the office, and it was enough to keep food on the table. I took a consulting job for an app start-up. I consulted for other businesses. I coached people who struggled with homeschooling. I coached relationships through rocky marriages. I attempted to teach online. Then my trauma brain flared up and I became depressed. The fear of losing everything again set in.

When we were approved for PPP, I went back to the treatment room to keep my business afloat and we reopened our doors on May 23. I was determined to keep us going. And although I was grateful, I missed the income and ease of teaching. I missed the impact and the interaction with others.

What if I could somehow bring the courses to my students? In October 2020, I launched the first Massage Therapy Continuing Education subscription box. I fought it out with the national board for approval. I ordered. I priced. I shopped. I planned. I prepped. My business had survived COVID19, but now it was my turn to make my heart full again.

I began the daunting task of trying to restaff to a capacity that would make it possible for me to return to teaching and helping others again. I loved the treatment room and my job there, but I felt I had the potential to make more of an impact outside of it. The confirmation came that it was time when I was interviewed by Women's Health Magazine.

I worked my way out of the treatment room and back into teaching. I began to hire more intentionally. I began to focus on leading more effectively. I put the people first knowing the money would follow. The story of how each individual came to be on my team in a market in which no one was showing for interviews is nothing short of divine intervention.

I let my frustrations fuel my future. I began to focus on being a leader in all areas of my life. I treated my staff like I wanted to be treated. From those circumstances, I have developed a team and a family beyond anything I ever could have dreamed of. I wouldn't trade them for the world.

• • •

Now I can say that everyday I am blessed to meet with clients who have been through what I have been through, and help them to keep sparkling. The past doesn't have to shine. We can still have a bright future ahead of us.

Sometimes life doesn't happen the way we expect. Sometimes God's plan is much greater than the one we have for ourselves, and He can do immeasurably more through us than we could have ever done by ourselves.

ASHLEY DWYER

Ashley Dwyer is a North Carolina Licensed Massage & Bodywork Therapist, NCBTMB Approved Continuing Education Provider, certified life, business and relationship coach and a certified small business consultant.

She published her first book, *Massage for Couples: Heal, Soothe and Connect with the One You Love*, with Rockridge Press in August 2020.

She has been featured in interviews with publications such as Women's Health Magazine and Hustle.

Her massage practice has won Best Massage Practice in Matthews-Mint Hill Weekly for 2019 and 2020, and she has also been nominated for Matthews-Mint Hill Weekly's Small Business Person of the Year for 2019 and 2020.

In her free time, she enjoys spending time with her son, Skyler, hiking, camping, gardening and caring for her cats, dog and chickens.

INVITATION FROM THE AUTHOR

Whether you're looking to heal your tired muscles or reignite your inner spark, I would love to invite you to contact us and schedule in your perfect hour of tranquility with a therapeutic massage. Can't wait to see you!

CONNECT WITH THE AUTHOR

Business Name: Fire & Ice Therapeutic Massage
Website: www.fireandicetherapeuticmassage.com
Facebook: www.facebook.com/fireandicemassage
Email: asdwyer2013@gmail.com

It's not about changing the world in a day, but taking small actions each day towards your goals. So take risks. Play BIG. Fall. Get back up. Celebrate the failures. Laugh. Grow. Inspire others. Be the BEST version of YOU. NEVER QUIT ON YOUR DREAMS!

Mariska Nagy

Frustrated, I exclaimed, "I feel the work we do is merely ticking a box, so the department can cover their arse!"

Knowing I had probably overstepped the line between robust conversation and directly questioning the integrity of our entire organisation, I waited for my director's response as he paused on the other end of the team call.

"You are right," he replied in a soft, almost defeated tone.

What! Did he really say that?

The entire team sat there in silence and looked at each other in astonishment and disbelief. I felt like he'd kicked us all in the guts, without him being physically present.

In just three little words, the seventeen years I'd committed to upholding our organisational values, the phone calls I'd fielded with complainants, cases I'd managed, reports I'd written, supervisors I'd seen broken by the system; they had all been questioned. In just three little words, I felt like my hard work and sacrifice had been reduced to nothing.

I didn't want much—just to feel the work I was doing made a difference. I wanted to feel a part of something bigger. I wanted to feel valued. Surely that wasn't too much to ask?

In that moment on that Monday morning, as I sat in the building which had become my second home, surrounded by the people who had become my friends, in a career I thought I would work in until the day I retired, and for a department I believed so strongly in, everything changed.

I knew this was a defining moment. I knew I couldn't stay.

But what was I going to do?

I couldn't just quit. I had poured almost two decades of my life into this career and I had a husband, two children and a mortgage. Damn it. I had responsibilities!

To top it off, I was part of one of Australia's last remaining defined benefits superannuation schemes. An enviable scheme which would set me up for a $2 million-plus retirement if I worked until I was sixty, and lived until I was one hundred (which was my plan). My logical brain was telling me that I'd be mad to quit.

I was conflicted to my core—the lure of a healthy retirement pension at the expense of my soul. So, I started to consider how I could earn the equivalent income and retire with $2 million by the time I was sixty, which was only fifteen years away. Despite my conflict I still wanted to retire and enjoy the wonderful, adventurous, nomadic life my husband and I had dreamed of. No biggie, right?

I am a strong woman. I am resourceful. I had always been a fighter who strived to see the positive in any challenge. I decided that I was not prepared to compromise my values because I wasn't only fighting for myself; I was fighting for my beliefs, my family, my future and my dreams.

My heart knew what I was looking for. Something I could do on *my* terms. Something that rewarded my efforts and paid me my worth. Something that didn't require a huge financial outlay or sacrificing too much time away from my family. Something that didn't require prior experience and which I could be mentored in.

So, I got to work and hit "Dr. Google".

I investigated every employment, recruiting, and investment website I could find. I researched how to start a traditional business, day trading, property investment, shares, crypto currency, Amazon selling, Shopify and more. I attended webinars that offered opportunities which were far too good to be true (minus the steak knives) and came up with a big fat zero!

Every opportunity I'd considered was either going to cost too much money or take up too much of my time and I didn't have much of either.

Just as I started to feel I would never find an answer, I received a phone call from my best friend, Anna. Anna told me that she had just started her own online business and invited me to take a look at it. Upon reflection, I don't know whether it was the vibe I was sending out to the universe, or Anna's eagerness to share what she had just discovered, but I knew I had nothing to lose in listening to what she had to say.

A few days later I met with Anna and her friend, Alexis, who had introduced her to the business. A social marketing business. Hmmm, not something I had considered in my quest for change, but something I was cautiously open-minded to learn more about.

I liked Alexis straight away. She was a straight shooter and, like me, had been looking for something more outside her career as a Police Detective. Her honesty was humbling. At first, she had been challenged by her own preconceived ideas about the social marketing industry. But, like any good detective, she investigated the company, the products, and the compensation plan. And, despite her own fear that an online social marketing business was way outside her comfort zone, she realized that she had absolutely nothing to lose and said yes to partnering with an established company and started her own business.

Alexis explained how she could run her business in the pockets of time she had between raising her two young daughters, juggling her and her husband's policing shifts, and expanding her investment property portfolio.

Flexibility. Tick.

She detailed the supportive community, and the training and mentorship she had received in building her business. She was in business for herself, but never by herself.

Support. Training. Mentorship. Tick. Tick. Tick.

She explained how the income she earned was effort based. If she chose to work her business, she got paid. If she chose not to work her business she wouldn't.

Paid for effort. Tick.

Then she explained the financial benefits: no need to create your own products or websites as these were provided by the company; no need to hold stock or deal with postage as this was also done by the company; no requirement to buy a "kit" to get started. The only mandatory requirement was the registration fee.

Minimal outlay. Bonus tick!

Alexis didn't have any experience running a business, but all the skills that were needed to be successful were learnable.

No experience needed. Tick.

I had learned skills before. I had learned to walk, talk, ride a bike, drive a car, be a parent, along with all the skills I'd learned from my previous jobs as a check out chick, a bank teller, a waitress, a student, a croupier, trainer and HR professional. This was no different.

Alexis revealed that while she had started her business for herself and her family, she quickly realized it wasn't all about her. She was now in the business of listening to and helping others create more for themselves.

As I listened to Alexis, my eyes widened, my heart beat a little faster, and my tummy fluttered. I became excited for the first time in what seemed like forever. I envisaged my family doing all the things we had only spoken about doing. Renovating our home, travelling, donating to charities close to our hearts, and setting up our kids.

"So how does it all work?" I asked.

The company she had partnered with sold over 450 consumable health and wellness products. Skin care, nutrition, bath and body products, hair care, cosmetics, and so much more. Non-negotiable items her family used every day.

Alexis had paid a small registration fee to become an independent consultant, received her own personalized website with the company and started buying her family's products online from her website. Instead of supporting the big corporations, she started supporting her own business.

With genuine excitement, Alexis explained how from day one she had shared this idea with others like me. Some had said yes to starting their own business, some had said no to starting a business but had purchased products from her website, and some people weren't interested in either.

This was a business in a box! The concept was genius and I couldn't wait to get home and tell my husband, Stuart, all about it!

On the drive home from our meeting, my head was reeling. I was excited about what my future looked like, but then fear took over and bellowed like a loud speaker in my head:

What are you doing? What are people going to think? You've never run a business before. You are too busy. You don't have money to start a business. You can't leave your job and superannuation for this!

And the noise persisted for the hour-long drive home.

When I got home, I was a combination of nerves and exhilaration. I excitedly blurted out everything Anna and Alexis had shared with me.

Stuart sat and listened, and when I came up for air he said, "If you want to do it, just do it!"

So, I paused and took a deep breath before ringing Anna and Alexis. "I'm in!" I told them with inspired determination.

> *"Sometimes the people around you won't understand your journey. They don't need to. It's not for them!"*
> — ANON

I couldn't wait to tell my family and friends that I had found the solution I was so desperately looking for. I envisioned they would be so excited for me. I could see their faces. They would be thrilled for my new venture, eager to show their support by purchasing their personal care products from my website. At least, that was what I thought. The reality was very different.

The next day, I rolled into work with a different outlook than the Monday a few weeks before. The nine-to-five grind no longer defined me, nor what I was capable of doing anymore. I'd searched for something more and something more found me.

People were filing into the office, shoulders slumped with a glum look on their faces. I wanted to grab them by the shoulders, shake them and scream:

"THERE IS MORE TO LIFE THAN THIS. THERE IS MORE!"

As I exited the elevator, I saw my friend Bec, and I was dying to tell her my news. I respected her as an operator and a friend. She was also a straight shooter, she LOVED quality products and a good bargain! This business would be perfect for her. I knew that we would have so much fun doing this together.

I found Bec standing by her desk. After some small talk about our weekends, I said, "I am so excited. I have just started my own business." However, before I even had an opportunity to explain how great she would be at it, how beneficial it would be to her and her family, and how we could do this together, she said, "I'm not interested," and walked away.

I was in shock at her response. There was no, "Good on you," or, "I am so happy for you," or even, "What is it all about?" Nothing. I couldn't believe it. And Bec wasn't the only one.

I had heard of "tall poppy syndrome" before. Was this what was happening? Surely not. These were people who loved me. Knew me. Respected me. Why weren't they happy for me and supporting me?

I was getting frustrated and confused by the rejection from some of those closest to me and started questioning myself and my decision. I remembered Alexis explaining her challenges with some of her family and friends when she first started her business, and how she made room for personal development each day to help her with challenges like these. She had joked, "This business is like a personal development course in disguise." And boy was she right.

For the first time in thirty years I decided to invest in myself and I read my first book. It took just ten pages each day to read it in a month. I also plugged into podcasts and audio books. My car transformed into a mobile university and the more I learned the more my world expanded. I couldn't believe I had allowed my potential to lay dormant for nearly three decades!

I started trusting my intuition, my gut feeling and what I wanted for my life. After hearing a quote by Jim Rohn, "You are the average of the five people you spend the most time with," I became aware of the people I was surrounding myself with. If I ever found myself around negativity I would visualise myself in a bubble filled with light and hope which could only be penetrated by those exhibiting positivity and support. I traded TV for training, and scrolling on social media for 'connecting' with people. Most of my life remained the same; I just made small changes which made a big difference!

At first some of these changes were foreign to me. I was a logical thinker and had never been into the "fluffy" style of thinking or learning. But as I travelled further into my PD journey, I was finding myself implementing a whole range of "woo woo", and it worked. As Stephen R. Covey says, "To achieve goals you've never achieved before, you need to start doing things you've never done before."

But my story and lessons did not end there.

> *"The greatest thing about being an entrepreneur is you are your own boss. The worst thing about being an entrepreneur is you are your own boss."*
>
> — ANON

I awoke each day with a fresh enthusiasm. I focussed on the people who had shown me support and was grateful for them. I was ready to share my story and authentically share with others how a social marketing business could help them too. Family, friends, colleagues, past associates. People who craved their own flexibility, who felt lost in their current careers and those who were seeking change. In my heart I *knew* I had a solution for them.

But I found myself lost and overwhelmed by the newfound freedom of working for myself. I had been an employee for over thirty years. I was used to being told what to do, what time I needed to be at work, what tasks I needed to complete each day. I was totally spoon fed and dependent.

I reached out to Alexis who offered me a few things I could do to bolster my self-belief.

I jumped onto the weekly training my team offered. I attended as many business presentations as I could, both in person and online. I knew that success left clues, so I followed the suggested daily method of operation (DMOs), which included goal setting, vision boards, journaling, affirmations, gratitude, manifesting, and a whole lot more.

As my knowledge expanded, I adapted my DMO so it worked for me and my family. I woke early, committed to my own mindset and belief through PD, gratitude, and affirmations, and then when the kids were dropped at school I was ready to work on my business.

My car was my classroom and office. As I drove between my job, home, shopping and kids' activities, I switched from listening to the radio to listening to audiobooks, podcasts and making team calls. I learned to utilize the small pockets of time, like my lunch break or arriving early to pick up the kids, to reach out to people and build my business. Small changes.

I involved my husband and kids, and together we created vision boards. It was important for me that they be connected to my vision because, despite my own personal desire for change, my long-term goal was to create lifestyle choices and freedom for them.

I followed industry leaders via social media, listened to their podcasts and read their books. These strangers (along with the people on my team) became my mentors and I couldn't get enough of their knowledge.

I followed their lead and momentum started to happen. I began registering clients and registering people to start their own business. I learned how to support and mentor them, sharing my story and how I'd learned from my mistakes, hoping my hindsight would be their foresight.

Despite the waves of momentum, the reality of business cycles started to kick in. Some months I'd be kicking goals, yet in others I'd lose my mojo. I catapulted between elevating to the next level in my business and then losing it.

I felt a growing feeling of uncertainty. At first, I struggled to pinpoint the cause. I had belief in the company, belief in the products, belief in the huge potential of the social marketing industry in this ever-changing world. But then I realized my lack of uncertainty wasn't about any of these things. This was much worse.

There was a place within me that felt I didn't deserve to have success and keep it.

I knew that the reason I wasn't maintaining my goals had way more to do with my beliefs about myself than it did with my capability to hit my goals. More importantly, I wasn't accomplishing my goals consistently because my inner programming was keeping me small, year after year. When I realized this, I became determined that the next twelve months were going to be very different from the previous twelve months which were plagued by self-limiting beliefs. I didn't want to just do things better; I wanted to be a better version of myself so I could grow into the person I needed to be to realize my goals and vision.

> *"Whether you think you can or think you can't, you are right."*
>
> — HENRY FORD

I realized it was time to get messy with myself and my past.

I doubled my daily PD with a focus on stories with grit, inspiration, and success. I surrounded myself with a new group of virtual mentors: Vishen Lakhiani, Jay Shetty, Simon Sinek, John C. Maxwell, Brené Brown, Dr. Carol Dweck, Esther and Jerry Hicks, Dr. Joe Dispenza. And I even started seeing a transformation and healing coach, who I work with to this day.

I am not going to lie. Some days are ugly. Tough. Like a scene from a Rocky movie. I often feel battered and bruised and there have been tears. Lots of tears.

The process is like sandblasting layers of paint that have been accumulated over decades to find who I am at my core. This deep, inward journey of mine is ongoing, but I remain inspired by what awaits me. I have the most amazing opportunity to build myself up based on what I want, who I want to be, and what I believe I truly deserve. And through my business, I have a vehicle through which I can inspire others to do the same.

"The journey of a thousand miles begins with one step."
— LAO TZU

All of my growth has taken time and will continue to do so. It's not about solving fifty years of ingrained encoding in a month. In our "never enough" society that is motivated by immediate gratification, most people expect to be transformed or achieve success overnight. But in reality, it is the small steps, small improvements, and small choices that compound and transform us over time.

Steve Jobs once said, "You can't connect the dots looking forward, so you have to trust the dots will somehow connect in your future."

Upon reflection, I can now connect the dots thus far. Starting my social marketing business led me to PD, which gave me the confidence to leave my career, which led me to being open to new possibilities, which led me to a bigger version of myself and in turn, has led me to write this chapter for you.

Did I think I would be here five years ago? No way! But it's funny how the universe works. I know life is happening FOR me, not TO me. I trust my intuition, am open to anything, and trust I am on the right path.

I finally have a feeling of freedom and this is just the beginning!

I am thankful for everyone who has supported me. I am even appreciative of those who chose not to (there is a lesson in everything). I love the gift of the social marketing industry. This business is a vehicle to do the things my husband and I only dreamed of. I love sharing this opportunity with others as a viable way out of any challenge they may be facing; from personal, health, or financial goals. In my heart I know I have a solution and I love mentoring people who decide to put themselves and their dreams first and start *their* own business. Most of all, I love seeing the look in their eyes when they achieve *their* goals. That's what it is all about.

> *"Don't be afraid to do something because you are scared of what others will think. They will judge you no matter what you do."*
>
> — ANON

So that's my story (to date). What's yours?

We all have the power within us to be an architect of our own lives. If you are reading this book, knowing you want MORE and are unsure of where to start, pat yourself on the back, as you have already started simply by reading these chapters.

If you are not where you want to be right now, only you have the power to change that. If that change is a priority, you will make it happen. If it's not, you will make excuses, procrastinate, and find blame.

Don't focus on, "What if it doesn't work," focus on, "What if it does work!" Don't fear failure (there is no such thing, only lessons to be learned), fear not trying.

My advice; Do your research. Invest in yourself. Find a mentor (even if they are authors of the books you read or the podcasts you listen to). Take a course. Follow your gut. Work smart, not hard. Take action each day towards your goals, even if it is small. Think about the legacy you want to leave and the example you want to be to others. Go to bed each night without an ounce of potential left in you.

As we know from recent world events, tomorrow is not promised to any of us. So, what are you waiting for?

ABOUT THE AUTHOR

MARISKA NAGY

Mariska Nagy is a social marketing professional, and a student and teacher of personal development. With prior careers in banking, hospitality and federal government, she understands the personal and financial challenges people face in today's busy world.

Mariska is passionate about helping others discover what is possible for them using the power of social marketing and has been mentored by several industry leaders. She enjoys working collaboratively with people, guiding them to be the best they can be through personal development and supporting them as they embark on starting and growing their own social marketing businesses.

Mariska attributes her continued personal and business development to an honest, consistent, and empathetic approach, and a genuine desire to serve others.

She currently lives and works in Melbourne with her husband and two children.

INVITATION FROM THE AUTHOR

Please visit my website to learn about how you can have more from life through personal development, an unwavering mindset and a passive income stream!

www.abetterwaywithmariska.com

CONNECT WITH THE AUTHOR

Business Name: A Better Way with Mariska
Website: www.abetterwaywithmariska.com
Facebook: www.facebook.com/abetterwaywithmariska
Email: abetterwaywithmariska@gmail.com

*When women connect
and collaborate, we
become a POWERHOUSE
of unstoppable ENERGY!*

Samantha Nichole

What happens when a narcissist and an empath walk into a bar? Google it, and an article by the Elephant Journal pops up. It's about the dynamics of abuse between the two, and how empaths (highly sensitive people who have the ability to sense what other people are feeling) and narcissists (those with a grandiose sense of self-importance and a deep need for excessive attention and admiration) have such dynamic dualistic qualities which make them so compelling to each other. For example, the empath admires the narcissist's intelligence and charisma, while the narcissist feeds off the unconditional love and support from the empath. "It is not just the narcissist that drives the paradigm, but the person he carefully selects to assist him" (Leibrandt, 2015). I didn't write the article, but it felt like it was speaking right to me. This was my story. The words I couldn't say myself flowed out from the page as if they were my own. I came to the understanding that I wasn't alone in this.

I just so happen to love elephants, and I'm also an empath, who in fact walked into a bar and met a narcissist. Crazy, right? These synchronicities are signs of the way the Universe (God, Spirit, Source Energy) speaks to me. From seeing 11:11 everywhere to déjà vu, vivid dreams and more, I have connected with Source Energy throughout my mind, body, and soul healing journey over the past four years.

The moment I met the narcissist my world was flipped upside down. It was the summer of 2011 and he swept me off my feet with dreams of a future together. We quickly moved into an apartment and I got pregnant. Unbeknownst to me, he was addicted to opioids. My motherly instinct kicked in and I went into overdrive trying to fix him. We lost that baby and I began falling deeper into what's called "trauma bonding". Experiencing trauma with someone who is unhealthy makes the situation worse. It's almost like I became emotionally addicted to him and the drama. I loved him through the addiction and the abuse. I wanted him to get better so we could live happily ever after.

We're sold the fairy tale dream from childhood; that our prince charming will come on a white horse and take us to our forever home in a castle. He had a nice car and still lived with his parents. The dream was to buy a house, but week after week we were spending more and not saving at all. Our actions were not in alignment with our dreams. He spent some time in rehab, and when he returned I got pregnant again, this time with twins.

I had always loved the idea of being home with my children and having a career that I was passionate about; something that makes an impact on my life, but also on the lives of others. I was introduced to direct sales and social media network marketing. I started working a side-hustle to make enough money to support myself. I was sharing products and my results, making friends from all over the world. We were sharing our stories and found the connections between us. It felt so good to not feel alone. I finally felt like there were other women like me who resonated with my pain and supported me, even if they were only a virtual BFF. There was something deep inside of me that wanted more out of life. I could feel the expansion in my bones. The eagerness to learn, experience and play with something new.

That fire in my belly was the catalyst for me to start a home-based business, even without any support from my boyfriend. "You can't run a business," he would say. I was only good enough to stay home and be a mother. I knew everything about the relationship was toxic and that fueled my fire to try harder and fix my life. One direct sales company after another I was failing, and he was right. The self-doubt weighed heavy on me. There was a huge disconnect between my own dreams and actions. Much like spending more than saving, I was doing everything out of desperation, and without belief.

Well, if you know anything about the law of attraction, then you know it's the emotions behind the desire that count. I didn't believe in myself. How could I when my environment wasn't set up for success? I would make a few sales here and there which showed me it was possible. But everyone doubted me, and I was slowly losing myself in the process. While I was living with him and his parents, raising our babies, the toxicity grew. The tension at the dinner table, being given the silent treatment. I felt like an outsider, always being judged and criticized. Everything I did was wrong to them. I was constantly walking on eggshells trying not to provoke anyone. "He doesn't hit me," I would tell my friend when she tried to reason with me. It wasn't that bad, I thought.

It wasn't until my friend introduced me to articles and videos about domestic violence that I started to recognize what was happening. I was enduring verbal, mental, and emotional abuse from my narcissistic boyfriend. I was treated like a child, made to feel small, unworthy, and I looked up to him as perfect and all knowing. I was being gaslighted and love-bombed month after month, fight after fight. There were more bad times than good times, and on my thirtieth birthday night it became physical. He assaulted me while we were out celebrating with my friends. The police came, and I begged them not to take him. "He didn't mean it! Really, we just want to go home," I said to them. Without pressing charges, they released us. I thought I was going to die that night as he drove us home drunk, yelling obscenities at me. Still, I didn't leave. I felt stuck. I had nowhere to go. No job, no money, nothing.

I went to a small mom's group at church a few months later. We were having a conversation and out of nowhere I expressed everything that I had been holding onto. I felt safe with them, in that sanctuary of hope and forgiveness. I let it all go, everything that had happened over the years. What happened next was incredible. Those women came together with their love and resources to help me to rise. Within minutes I was on the phone with social services, and a few hours later I had a temporary protective order. The shift had arrived. I still remember the disbelief as I awakened to what was happening.

In a tiny cold room, I sat with a case worker, answering questions like, "Has he ever threatened you with a weapon? Do you think he might try to kill you? Does he have a gun? Is he violent or constantly jealous or does he control most of your activities?" I replied, "Yes, yes, yes and yes." Wow. How did I not realize it was this bad? How did I think this was normal? The next few days were a blur. I quietly packed my things. I moved out two days later with a safety escape plan in place. My children and I stayed with my parents, back in my old bedroom. We were there for a year while I got back on my feet. I started looking for jobs, exercising more, and eating healthier.

I landed a part time job working as a personal assistant for a self-made millionaire in direct sales and network marketing. She was my idol. I wanted everything she had, and I was finally submersed in an environment where I could learn and grow—her home office. I was excited for my future for the first time in years.

But even though I had a great opportunity in the role, I wasn't succeeding fast enough and needed a full-time job to supplement my income. I was happy to land a nine-to-five office job. I worked so hard to learn the basic skills of interviewing again: making eye contact is a big deal for victims of domestic abuse. I'd worked office jobs before, but after years of abuse, I was just not myself anymore. I couldn't handle constructive criticism; I was triggered tremendously. I used to be great at multitasking, a rock star at balancing under pressure, but this time it felt overwhelming. I was diagnosed with PTSD, anxiety, and depression after leaving that relationship. Fighting between the dreams in my mind and the reality of my scars proved to be difficult during this time of growth. I quit the part-time job and focused on building my savings so I could move out of my parent's house.

During this time, I became immersed in personal development. I read books and watched online content of highly successful people. I challenged my mindset daily and started speaking words of affirmation. Soon after, I met the man of my dreams. He was pursuing his career, mindful of a healthy lifestyle, and had lots of hobbies. We chatted about exercising and having a positive mindset. We met for coffee and shared our pasts (that's what you do after 30-something, just get it all out there!). Turns out, we had a lot in common and the connection was wild. I had to have more of his energy around me; I craved a human like this. Sensitive and strong. Hard working and down to earth. Honest and caring. He was everything that I was trying to attract into my life.

In her book, *You Can Heal Your Life*, Louise Hay talks about mirror work, and the idea is that you speak to yourself in the mirror with specific gratitude's of accomplishment in advance. THE LAW OF ATTRACTION IS REAL! I was healing and it showed, not only in my external world, but my inner world as well. I believed in myself. I knew what I wanted, and I was going after it with passion and on purpose. I moved out of my parent's home and we bought a house together, exactly one year on from the day I left my abuser. The signs and synchronicities were presenting themselves again.

The year grew into homeownership and cohabiting in a healthy relationship. But there remained triggers from my past that I still needed to work through. I would pick fights for no reason, emotionally addicted to the drama. I had to catch myself by becoming aware and showing myself love and compassion. I still needed to heal. I was put on prescription medications and plugged into the system as a victim of domestic violence. It seemed like all my hard work was going down the drain as my mental health deteriorated.

I started researching natural ways to approach my health and well-being. Around every corner, legal cannabis and medical marijuana kept popping up. I had tried it once in high school and hated it, never touching it again until my ex introduced it to me. I didn't understand the difference between drugs and plant medicine, but when I tried it with my ex, I was certainly happier. We had used it as a crutch, however, abusing it daily. But since I had left him and the negativity behind me, I knew it could now work for me in a healthy way. I didn't want the high, only the health benefits from the plant. That's when I found hemp and CBD. Different from the marijuana plant, CBD from hemp doesn't get you high, but gives you all the benefits. I attended a local women's wellness event and learned about the different uses, benefits, how to cook with it, and more. I met women from all different backgrounds with diverse stories and different reasons as to why they were choosing plant medicine.

I searched online and found a company that farmed and sold hemp in the US legally. It was a direct sales and network marketing company. I knew this would be the start of another new beginning for me. On my thirty-second birthday, I began my holistic wellness journey with CBD oil and within three months I had successfully weaned myself off the seven daily pills the doctors were prescribing me. I no longer felt like a zombie. I felt like myself. I was happier, more focused, less anxious. Month after month, I noticed other things improving: my sleep, my menstrual cycle, my thought processes, and for the first time ever I was feeling creative and inspired to share my journey. I started the CBD business by networking, talking to new people about my experience, documenting my new healthy lifestyle, educating myself, and sharing it all on social media.

My story had a ripple effect. Whenever I would share my story on a livestream I met new friends with similar stories. Within a few months I had built a team and following of other women who were inspired by my story and wanted to try a more natural approach to their health and wellness. And so began my entrepreneurial journey.

Showing up on social media with such personal details and aspirations can be quite daunting. Let's face it, we care about what other people think of us, and as much as I was scared I knew this was my opportunity to not only get healthier and take back control of my life but to free myself from fear of judgement and regret. I went all in. I empowered myself and was more consistent than I had ever been.

Word spread that I was on this wellness journey with cannabis and my ex tried to take the kids from me claiming I was using drugs. Child protective services came to investigate. I stood my ground even though

I was afraid. I believed in myself and the path I had chosen. I fought back. I spoke my truth even when my voice was shaking. I was not a bad mom for using cannabis instead of prescription drugs, but there were others who disagreed with me.

There were no findings of illegal drug use, so the case was dropped and I continued to grow my business online, meeting even more women and empowering, inspiring, and uplifting them to make bold moves and stand in their truth. After a year working the business, I hit the top one percent on the leaderboard! I qualified for extra bonuses and received an award. I built an international team of women and mothers from all over the world who were inspired by my resilience and passion for natural living. We became a powerhouse together, co-creating ideas, putting out valuable pieces of inspirational content, sharing our success stories online that empowered even more women!

I invested in courses to become a certified life coach and meditation teacher, working with energy and using tools of transformation for mind, body, and soul healing. As I deepened my own practice, I started my own small business and took my career to the next level. I created a company and built a community, and began offering coaching services, workshop programs, and wellness products. CBD is such a huge part of my business. At the start of a meditation class we drop our CBD oil and ground our energy with relaxing music and essential oils.

I am so glad I didn't quit, even when it all felt too hard. I am so grateful for the resilience in my passion to pursue my happiness which sets my soul on fire. We all have dreams. They may look different and we may share different stories; but if we connect and collaborate, our energy is contagious.

SAMANTHA NICHOLE

Samantha Nichole began her journey of self-healing, self-love and self-growth after leaving an abusive relationship. She created Mindful Mama Holistic Wellness to help empower and inspire women who are healing from unhealthy relationships.

She is a certified life coach, meditation teacher and Reiki practitioner. Samantha is currently facilitating breathwork and meditation classes, workshops and offering one-on-one and group coaching programs online and in her Reiki studio.

Samantha and her manifested man live in their dream home in Southern Maryland, raising three awesome kids: twins and a teenager. They love to travel and explore outdoors while vlogging their adventures.

INVITATION FROM THE AUTHOR

I hold space and create containers with women who are ready to rise! From one-on-one intimate sessions to group coaching programs and multiple day workshops, there is always something exciting and available to reignite your energy and activate your Higher Self. Weekly breathwork and meditation classes are available online. My signature course is called Your Higher Self awaits you! Visit: https://calendly.com/mindfulmamaxo or find me on social media.

CONNECT WITH THE AUTHOR

Business Name: Mindful Mama Holistic Wellness
Website: www.mindfulmamaholisticwellness.com
Facebook: www.facebook.com/samanthaxonichole
Email: mindfulmamaxo@gmail.com

A beautiful life comes from knowing your purpose and living it every day.

Abby Mason

It's August 1989 and I'm leaving for college. I'm heading to The University of Alabama. I'm nervous and excited at the same time. I can't stop thinking about this next chapter in my life. Will I get homesick? Will my expectations be met through this experience?

Our car is loaded, and the U-Haul is attached to the back filled with everything I'm going to need in my new life. I say goodbye to my childhood friends and hit the road. Tears fill my eyes as my parents and I drive away. The windows are down, and I can smell the sweet scents of lilies and irises in bloom. I'm going to miss home.

We arrive in Tuscaloosa, Alabama and the campus is full of students already. I feel a little overwhelmed. I wonder if I made the right decision to study so far from home? When I am finally all moved in I hug my parents goodbye. Tears again fill my eyes. I feel so alone suddenly. But sorority rush week starts tomorrow. I have all my outfits picked out and I am ready to do this!

I go through the rush process and it's emotionally and physically exhausting. I find my new family as I pledge Alpha Omicron Pi. I meet some amazing girls and am so excited for these new friendships. There are so many events: date nights with the fraternities, charity projects, football games, and social engagements with other sororities. Our next event is with the Sigma Chi fraternity.

I walk into the venue with three of my closest sorority sisters. My eyes immediately lock on this guy standing across the room with a bunch of his fraternity brothers. We walk over to them and start chatting. His name is Justin and there is instant attraction between us. We talk for what seems like hours and are the last to leave.

Justin is eight years older than me, in his senior year, and is from Fort Lauderdale. He joined the Marines after high school and then enrolled at The University of Alabama. We start dating. He says all the right things and treats me like a princess. We adore each other.

But as each month passes, he becomes a little more controlling and possessive. I sense that something is not right and wonder if I should try to break it off and get some space, but I can't muster up the courage to do it. I know it would break his heart. We continue to date for the rest of my freshman year. It's now May 1990. I decide to move to Fort Lauderdale with him and just hope I have made the right decision.

I stay with my aunt and uncle in Coral Springs which is close to Justin's parent's home. I get a job leasing apartments on a beautiful property. I am so excited about the opportunity and I love my job. Soon, I'm able to move out of my aunt and uncle's into a gorgeous two-bedroom apartment on the property where I am the leasing specialist. I decide that I like it here and start to wonder if I want to go back to Alabama for college.

Justin tries to convince me to stay and go to school in Florida because he wants to finish school here. I'm not sure what I want but I know I don't want to be far from him.

Most of our time together is spent hanging out with his friends. I notice that Justin is becoming more distant from me. He isn't as affectionate as he once was and his tone of voice has changed, his words have become mean. Is it because his friends don't care for our relationship? Does he want to break up? My heart and mind are all over the place. I want to go back to Alabama for my sophomore year. Every time I try to distance myself from him, he says he's sorry and pulls me back in with stronger affection and all the right words.

He stays over at my apartment most nights. The relationship is strained, and he becomes more distant with each day. Tonight, something seems off when he gets back from hanging out with his friends. I ask him about the way he's acting, and he says he had too much to drink. I toss and turn all night with frustration. Something just isn't adding up.

In the morning, I ask him again what he did last night? He finally admits he went on a date with someone his friend hooked him up with. My heart sinks to the floor with devastation. Tears immediately flow from my eyes. How can this be happening? I ask him to leave straight away. I call my dad and tell him I can't stay in Florida anymore. The realization hits me that I've been miserable for months.

My dad and I decided I should move back to Ohio and enroll at Ohio State University. Justin and I have a long heart to heart and we agree to break up. We know we're not meant to be together and we're both miserable. It's now August and my dad arrives to take me home. As we pull away I feel relief and know that I have made the right decision.

On the drive home I do some soul-searching. I decide to make my life my priority and pour myself into my schoolwork at OSU. I start my classes in September 1990. I meet new friends and reconnect with old ones from my high school who also go here. I'm enjoying my subjects and my grades are thriving.

In mid-October I realize I am two months late in my cycle. I decide to get a pregnancy test, hoping that it's just a mistake. But it's POSITIVE! This cannot be happening, I tell myself. What will become of my future? I know the baby is Justin's, but should I tell him?

I spend weeks going back and forth deciding what to do. I finally confide in my sister and she says I need to tell our mom and dad. She assures me they will be supportive. This is one of the most difficult things I have ever had to do in my life.

I sit them down on our patio and I show them the ultrasound. Everyone begins to cry. Waves of emotions flow through us. They both hug me, and we talk and cry for what seems like half the day. They tell me they will help me get through this and they encourage me to tell the father.

I pick up the phone, my hands shaking. He answers, and I can hardly speak through the tears. We talk for about two hours and finally decide that, despite everything, it's better that we stay broken up. He's not sure what he wants to do in his role as a father. He says he needs time to process it all.

I feel glad that he doesn't want to be together, but then this feeling of loss overtakes me. What in the world have I done to my life and my future? I'm only nineteen years old. How could I have been so stupid and careless? I'm so ashamed of myself and it's one of the lowest points in my life.

In late November, Justin calls me. He has decided he wants to be part of our child's life. We discuss in length if we should get married. I'm skeptical because we didn't get along when we were just dating, but my parents are pushing me to get married. I can tell they are ashamed of me; I see it in their eyes. They feel this is the only solution, but I'm torn, and I don't know what the right decision is.

It is getting close to the holidays and Justin is coming to visit. I'm three months pregnant and not showing at all. I wonder what will come of this visit? I'm having second thoughts. I don't want him to come. I wish I'd never gone to Florida. I wish I'd chosen to come back to Ohio for the summer.

It's a cold December day. There's snow all over the ground. The fireplace is going strong in the family room and the scent of burning wood fills the air. It's time to head to the airport to pick Justin up. I wonder what it will be like to see him after all these months? I'm so nervous. My heart races and I feel like I'm going to faint.

But at the sight of him coming through the doors towards me my heart instantly melts. I wasn't expecting it. He runs to me and we hug for what seems like forever. All my doubts disappear. We go out to dinner and spend hours talking about what is best for us and the baby. He admits he didn't treat me well when we lived in Florida and he promises to do better and treat me like I deserve. He says he wants to be with me, to give us a second chance.

It's two days later. We get in the car to go out for a nice dinner. I feel like we're getting closer again and our connection is growing. He asks me to get his driver's license from the sun visor above me. That's a strange place for a driver's license, I think to myself. I reach to pull the visor down and an engagement ring falls into my lap.

I'm at a loss for words, my whole body shaking. He asks me to marry him and I say yes. We agree that we want to become a family and that it's the best thing for our child. The wedding planning is underway, and we set the date for March 2 1991. With his love and support I finally believe that this really could work.

We get married on a beautiful Spring day. All the planning paid off and it goes perfectly. I feel like I'm falling back in love with him. He is more attentive and considerate. He is taking care of me the way I had always hoped he would. It's just like it was when we first started dating. Our baby is due on May 26 and we're getting excited for her arrival.

It's May 13 1991, and during our nightly walk I start to experience strong contractions. I call my doctor and he says to go to the hospital. This is it! This is happening.

She arrives at 4:41 a.m. My sweet baby girl is here. This is a dream. I have my little family. This baby is going to be the glue that keeps Justin and I together and I just know we're going to have an amazing life.

Our daughter, Maria, is now three months old. I'm exhausted from lack of sleep and constantly attending to her. Justin is becoming more distant. He's always out with his friends and doesn't seem to want to spend time with us. My heart is breaking. The reality that I made the wrong decision to get married is overwhelming, but I feel trapped. What have I done! I never should have told him I was pregnant.

It's a Saturday and Summer is in full bloom. The windows are open and the fresh air fills the house. I hear Maria cooing in her crib through the monitor. It's just about time for her to fall asleep for her nap. I ask Justin if we can have a talk, a serious one.

I'm miserable, I tell him. We argue constantly, and I've had enough. He says he is miserable as well. He hates living in Ohio and wants us to move back to Florida. He promises me that things will be better there. I am hesitant, thinking about the first time we moved there from Alabama, but he assures me this is best for our family.

I finally agree and in the blink of an eye we are on the road. We have picked out a lovely apartment and I try to convince myself that it's going to be perfect. It's for our daughter. We are going to be a better family in Florida.

The road trip seems to take forever. I spend many quiet moments during this car ride contemplating my life's decisions. The "would haves", "could haves", and "why did I's" are playing very loud in my mind. It is late at night now and we are getting close to our new home. The windows are down, the air is warm. I feel a wave of emotion sweep through my heart and tears pour out of my eyes. I look out the window so he can't see the sadness on my face.

We settle into our new life and things quickly go from bad to worse.

We are fighting more than ever, and he seems to be very taken with a girl from work. I spend each day caring for our daughter and trying to build a life with him. I feel so alone, and I am emotionally drained. I begin to journal again each morning. I used to do this in high school.

I had no one to talk to and I was really struggling to make sense of life and all the stress around me. Journaling helped me get my thoughts on paper. It gave me a sense of release and almost a sense of stability and resiliency. I once again feel as if I have no one to talk to. All my friends are in college and wouldn't understand. I can't live this way. I have my whole life ahead of me and I don't want to raise my daughter in this environment. The verbal abuse is unbearable. We argue about anything and everything and he is constantly calling me the most vulgar names. He puts me down so much that I feel like I am lower than the dirt on the ground.

His parents take us out to dinner every Wednesday night to help us navigate our relationship. We tell them that we just don't get along. We don't even like each other anymore. I am wondering if we ever did. We finally decide that Justin and I need to get a divorce.

Here I am again faced with another awful life decision. I'm twenty-one years old, with a one-year-old, and about to become a single mom. I feel like a complete failure. I have let myself down, my family, and my daughter. I can't give her the life she deserves. A happy family with her father is not in her future.

It is now June 1992. I'm living with my dad and desperately searching for a job. I need to be able to support myself and Maria. I am so grateful that my dad is letting us live with him. I don't know what I would do without his support. We have a very good relationship. He is great with Maria, and she adores her papa.

I go to job interview after job interview with no luck. I decide to get my real estate license after a friend asks me to work with her as her assistant. I get my license and as soon as I pass my exam she lets me know that she doesn't need an assistant after all. What do I do now? I have interviews with several realtors hoping one of them will want me to be their assistant. Without success.

It is a fall afternoon and I am laying on the couch in the family room sobbing. Maria has just laid down for her afternoon nap. The room is quiet and empty. There is only this couch and a television. I lay there looking out the open patio doors watching the leaves fall from the trees. The air is crisp and a little chilly. I get up and walk to the open door. I take a deep breath and breathe in the scent of the fall aroma outside. There is just something about the air when it is cooler, and the leaves when they change and begin to fall from the branches.

But I'm so scared about my future. How can I take care of my daughter if I can't find a job? Everyone is looking for a college graduate, and I threw that away. What is going to become of my future? I am broken. I am at my lowest low.

Then, the phone rings. It's one of the realtors I interviewed with a month ago. He says he wants to hire me. The timing of his call is incredible, I tell him, laughing and crying at once. He tells me I can start right away.

I get settled and I do well with my career as a real estate assistant. I enjoy working with the realtor and his wife. They are so good to me. The pay is good, and I finally feel like there is hope for the future.

My daughter and I are now living in our own apartment. I feel proud of myself for the first time in as long as I can remember. But at the same time, I'm lonely, and at night I lie awake wondering if I will ever be able to find someone who would want to be with a single mom.

Real estate is a tough job. There are lots of moving parts, but I pour myself into becoming a perfectionist at my work. I want to become a realtor on my own. I continue to find success, but I notice my energy being drained. I wonder if I can go on feeling this way, but in reality I have no choice. What else could I possibly do except dream of ways to get out of real estate and find a career I love.

It takes a year for Justin to finally sign the divorce papers and by now I'm ready to date again. I go on several dates but none that I want to pursue. It's June 18 and a beautiful Saturday evening. Friends and I go to a bar that has great live music. It's here that I run into a childhood crush. We start talking and connect instantly. His name is Andrew, and it turns out he is the sweetest man I have ever met.

We date for two years. In August 1995 we are on a beach in Sarasota, Florida. It's here that he asks me to marry him. In April 1996 we are married in Hawaii. We want to start a family right away. And with the money I am making as a realtor, I can put the down payment on our first house.

Our first daughter is born on June 29 2000. Andrew and I decide that I will quit work as a realtor and become a stay-at-home mom. He tells me that when I am ready to go back to work he will support me in whatever passion I want to pursue.

It's now June 2014. We have two more daughters, so four children in all. Our youngest is starting first grade and it's time for me to find a career I love. Over the years I have poured my free time into learning about health and wellness which has always been a passion of mine. Could I make this a career? Friends have always told me that I'm a good listener, that they can always come to me for support when they've struggled in life.

So, I enroll in the Institute for Integrative Nutrition. This certification program teaches over one hundred dietary theories and a variety of practical lifestyle coaching methods. Some of my favorite wellness warriors, such as Deepak Chopra, Mark Hyman, Frank Lipman, Gabby Bernstein, and Latham Thomas, are teachers in this course.

I want to be that support system for other women when they are struggling with life's challenges. This has always been a dream of mine, tracing back to my high school years when I felt I had no one to turn to. I am finally going to do what I love.

I became certified in 2015 and my health coaching business is off and running. I have a handful of women that I am coaching to improve their overall health and wellness. In 2016, I join a chiropractic wellness center as its certified integrative nutrition health coach. It is a beautiful facility and I have a steady stream of clients each week.

I listen authentically to my clients as they share their hopes, struggles and goals. And I provide a safe and judgement-free space. I come to work every day with excitement knowing I can make a difference in someone's life. Witnessing the positive transformation in these women is truly a gift to me.

As I reflect on my journey and the challenges that I have faced over the years, I accept them as life's lessons to truly appreciate where I am today. I have the family that I have always wanted and a career I have always dreamed of. I started in my early twenties as a lotus flower in the depths of the mud and muck below the water. Today I have emerged with my head above water, living my best life. Life is beautiful.

• • •

If you can relate to my personal struggles or if my story has resonated with you, I would love for you to reach out to me. It would be my pleasure to support you and be someone with whom you can share your truth, struggles, and goals in life.

You are so unique in your own way, and there is no one-size-fits-all when it comes to lifestyle, nutrition, and mindset. These are the core of what makes you the best of who you are.

I believe now more than ever that you can benefit from talking to someone who can help navigate the murky waters of life so that you can live your purpose and become your own version of a lotus flower.

ABBY MASON

Abby Mason is the founder of Passionate Wellness and Rain4est Essentials Skin Care.

Abby offers custom skincare programs with formulations based on a client's ancestry.com and toolboxgenomics.com results. She coaches her clients to understand how to have flawless skin bio-individually through nutrition, lifestyle, and mindset.

Her focus is on hormone imbalance and digestive and absorption issues to uncover root causes of skin concerns. Knowing the root cause provides a roadmap for radiant, healthy skin and a robust immune system.

Abby is an AADP Board Certified Integrative Nutrition Health Coach, Functional Medicine Health Coach in Training, Advanced Skin Sequencing Practitioner, Certified Nutritional Aesthetics Practitioner, and Author.

As a graduate of the Institute for Integrative Nutrition, she trained in over one hundred dietary theories and a variety of practical lifestyle coaching methods.

She has been featured in Brainz Magazine and Shoutout LA.

INVITATION FROM THE AUTHOR

If you want to achieve timeless glowing skin through nutrition, life-style, and mindset, please contact me at healthcoachabbymason@gmail.com for a free 30-minute skin wellness consultation. You will receive three unique steps to get started right away!

CONNECT WITH THE AUTHOR

Business Name: Passionate Wellness
Website: www.abbymason.com
Facebook: www.facebook.com/wellnessabby
Email: healthcoachabbymason@gmail.com

As long as the Creator gives us breath, our destiny has not yet been fulfilled. We must honor that gift by creating value every single day.

Isabelle Aubé

The farther back you pull a bowstring, the further the arrow goes.

It's 2015. I was living in social housing with my two youngest daughters: unemployed, in family court with their father, and with no electricity. I remember crying at night pleading to the Creator to help me get out of this mess. How did someone like me get into this situation?

There were days when I thought God must have been punishing me for my sins from a previous life. How could a woman who always strived to do the right thing for her children and her community be subject to such horrible circumstances? I always looked to help others. Where did I go wrong? Was it true that no good deed goes unpunished?

It took me some years to understand that this victim mentality was exactly what got me into these predicaments in the first place. There must always be a villain to confirm the victim narrative playing out in the mind. As they say, we find the weapon to fit the wound. And if we do not heal that wound, it will inevitably bleed into every area of our lives.

I know this because it happened to me. And now I help others get out of these same nasty unconscious patterns that keep us trapped in painful and unhealthy situations.

Allow me to provide you with some context before I jump to the punchline.

My name is Isabelle Aubé, and I am the youngest of nine children. Born and raised in Canada, my family is of mixed heritage: Mi'kmaq, Algonquin, and French, with some English blood thrown in to complete the cocktail. Although I grew up with Indigenous art on our walls, braids in my hair and being called "savage" by some of the neighborhood kids, my family was mostly assimilated into mainstream society and identified primarily as French Canadian. It wasn't until my late teens that I was actively involved in the Indigenous community.

My parents were together for thirty-two years before they separated when I was fifteen. The marriage was already in trouble when I was born. My mother said my father was unfaithful and my father said my mother was immature and prone to exaggeration. The house always felt divided and tense.

However, I must also outline the good things that contributed to my success:

1. Hard work was always valued in my family.
2. Sport and physical activity were part of our daily lives.
3. My father always told me I was smart enough and capable enough to succeed at anything I set my sights on.
4. I had a supreme mother. She raised her nine kids and babysat eleven others for years at a time and started the cub scout movement in our neighborhood.
5. My father was very dedicated to us. And although strict, he taught us values and spirituality while being present in our lives.

Now that you are aware of my primary wounds and foundational values, let me tell you part of my tale ...

As they say, hindsight provides twenty-twenty vision. And in the early 2000s I met the weapon to fit my wounds.

Jim was not the person I thought he was when we first met. There were so many reasons not to stay with him, and I was actually going to leave him the day I found out we were having twin girls a year into the relationship.

My two oldest children were eight and five years old. I knew that there was no way that I could handle two kids plus twins as a single mother. So, I stayed.

It all came to a head in 2006 when I found out he was seeing one of his clients. To add insult to the injury I also found out that he had been storing large amounts of money away for himself while I covered his bounced cheques. So I ended it for good this time.

There I was, a single mom of four kids, running a fitness business that I had started a year earlier. I had twenty-five client sessions a week, taught personal training, ran fitness instructor and pre/postnatal fitness certification courses on the weekends, and taught in the sport management program at a local college. I never had to look for clients or any type of income as opportunities found me. I was featured in magazines, did television interviews. Despite Jim, life was good!

But by 2009, I was burnt out. The frantic pace at which I had been living had taken its toll. So, in July of that year, we moved cities and I got a position as a manager of sport/coaching at the Canadian National Equestrian Federation. Jim lived and worked in this city too. We went from living two hours away from Jim, to thirty minutes away. Little did I know how much the distance between us had provided a buffer for his chaos.

Once an entrepreneur, always an entrepreneur! By 2012 I decided to start another business. This one combined my skills and experience with my passion for sport and Indigenous health. I created a six day course that I called the Aboriginal Community Warrior Program. In this course, Indigenous community members received four days of a national personal training certification, one day of long-term athlete development training, and one day of community mobilization training. Over the course of three years I trained 230 people across Canada in my program.

The height of success for this business came when I was asked to present at the World Indigenous Health Conference to be held in Australia. I received a personal note from the selection committee telling me that I would be a highlight of the conference. It felt to me as if I had arrived! I would have international recognition and could grow my program in other countries. But I was never able to go to the conference.

From 2008 to the day he died of cancer in 2012, my father had been "managing" Jim. In 2008, my children went to visit him for the weekend. After getting into an argument with my eldest daughter, Jim thought it would be good parenting to drop off a fourteen-year-old girl on a country road in the middle of nowhere, with no cell phone, in a strange city. It was then that my father intervened and kept an eye on Jim through regular contact.

I didn't realize how much my father was protecting my children until after he died, and Jim spun out of control.

When we moved to the same city as Jim in 2009, the visitation arrangement was that my kids would go to Jim's every other week. In those weeks I would take a plane to wherever in Canada I was teaching my course for six days, and fly back home on Friday in time to greet my kids at the bus stop.

Jim's behavior became progressively worse. I would receive tearful calls from my daughters while with their father. The school would call to inform me that they were being sent to school without proper clothing in winter or having adequate food in their lunches.

The last straw happened in January of 2014. I listened in shock as my daughters told me how Jim had violently laid his hands on one of them while his new partner filmed my daughter's reaction.

Once I had the unwavering facts from my girls, I emailed Jim and informed him that he had twenty-four hours to provide me with his plan to get professional help. He didn't. So, I filed a custody case at the family courts and opened a file at our city's Children's Protection Agency.

Many court dates ensued. It was heartbreaking that my children no longer felt safe at their father's. I felt torn between providing for my children by traveling for work and staying home to protect them.

Over the next few years there were good court outcomes and bad court outcomes. In the end, I received full custody of the daughter Jim had offended. The problem now was that I couldn't travel to work, as she was with me full-time. And the courts did not adjust child support or the government child supplement until much later.

No longer able to travel, I had no viable income and exorbitant lawyer fees. Unable to pay my bills, our hydro was cut off for two weeks, and I had to go to the foodbank to feed us. It was utterly humiliating.

What got us through those years was soccer. My daughters started playing competitively at the age of twelve and I was their team's coach. I fell in love with the game and poured every moment I could into furthering my knowledge and skills. I studied every coaching certification course available to me. It didn't matter what was going on in our personal lives. As long as we could play soccer, it was a good day!

If it was going to be, it was up to me! Born with a fierce determination, I never gave up. This was not how my life was going to stay. Through a social assistance program I was able to get some financial help to pay off my utility bills.

The court cases concluded. Now my girls were with me full-time and child support was deducted right from Jim's paycheck. Even though this provided some financial stability, I then had a choice to make. Either I could pour every penny I made into paying off my lawyer fees and every other expense I had accumulated, or file for bankruptcy and invest all my money into keeping my kids in competitive sport.

I decided to take the financial hit and keep my daughters playing competitive soccer and futsal. Futsal is comparable to indoor soccer, except it is played in a gym with half the players and twice the speed. All the best soccer players in the world played futsal, and I had fallen in love with coaching the sport.

I managed to get a few contracts here and there and was finally able to move out of social housing in 2017. My daughters were starting high school and there they joined the school's soccer team. I attended their games, and was dismayed at the level of coaching. I approached the school's principal and offered my coaching services for both soccer and futsal.

In 2018, I coached the grade seven and eight boys and girls soccer and futsal teams into success. The boys team won the school's first championship banner and the girls were not far behind. In 2019 we did even better and they gave me the senior boys soccer team as well. In futsal the boys team dominated, winning every game and the gold medal. When I told one of my contacts who worked for a futsal organization in the United States, he invited us to play in the first ever School Futsal World Cup at the ESPN Sports Center in Orlando, Florida in July 2019. I was so excited to tell my players!

An important fact: I needed the school's permission to travel with the team. They informed me that they would not support the outing, but that I could register the team as a community team instead. I was disappointed. I had seven weeks to raise thousands of dollars to bring my team to this international competition.

If you tell me I can't do something that I know will help kids, I will do everything in my power to make it happen anyway!

I lost most of my players, as the parents didn't have the couple thousand dollars to put towards the unplanned trip. However, I managed to get six new players and we fundraised until a few days before departure.

Twice a week I taught the new team how to compete against the world! At the World Cup, we played Brazil for the gold medal, and lost. I am very proud to say that we were the only team who scored against the winner, and their coach admitted that we were the hardest team to beat. I was inspired. I felt I was good at this and I loved every single second.

When I returned, I spoke to the local futsal club about training athletes for international competitions and was shut down, just as many women who are up and comers in the sports world are shut down. I then approached our soccer club to offer them the same thing and they replied that they were not ready for this type of program.

So, I founded Elite Futsal Canada in early 2020, my own organization that would provide opportunities to players to compete in international competition, with me as the head coach.

March 13 2020, the pandemic hit and all sport was suspended. Like everyone else in the world, I had to pivot, and took my team training online. We had already paid the registration fee to play in the World Futsal Showcase/Championships in July of 2020. As time went on it became apparent that we couldn't compete and had to prepare to play in July of 2021 instead.

Although I had reinvented myself professionally, personally I was struggling. My thyroid had given out and as my weight increased my self-esteem tanked and I started hiding from public interactions aside from soccer and futsal activities. I felt locked into a loop of resentment, anger, victim mentality, and was very critical of myself.

The catalyst came when I visited my mother one day and met her cleaning lady. You know when you meet someone and get a great vibe from them? That was her. Within minutes I found out why. She told me that she was a clairvoyant and asked if she could give me a message. An avid tarot card reader like my mother, I said yes without hesitation. She told me that I needed to release my sadness as great things were waiting for me as soon as I did. I started crying right away and replied that I didn't know how. She advised me to light a white candle every day and to ask the Creator for help in releasing my burdens. That was the day that my life started to change.

Lighting that white candle everyday lifted the first level of depression. It helped me remember things I had learned years ago that I then combined and applied to my own healing. As a certified lifestyle coach with NLP (Neuro-Linguistic Programming) training from Dr. Richard Bandler himself, I had the tools I needed to put those horrid years behind me and change my mindset. I started using the moon cycles again to manifest and to release. I used EFT (Emotional Freedom Technique) to release trauma and limiting beliefs. My intuition came back tenfold, and things started falling into place. In November of 2020 I started my lifestyle coaching company called Native Way Coaching Services. One hour after I sent out the poster I received a call from an organization and filled up my week with sessions for their staff.

If that wasn't enough, I was approached by a magazine in Sweden about an award. I didn't think much of it until the list of honorees came out. On it were Elon Musk, Jim Kwik, Kamala Harris, Greta Thunberg among many other respected Leaders.

The techniques and hard work I put into getting unstuck worked. I am now happier than I have ever been and only getting started.

I am still training my elite Futsal team three times a week, and we make training videos that I post to Facebook and Instagram every Sunday. We have a minimum of 70k to 150k views a week with many messages from players who want to come to Canada to play for us.

Sport is one of the best therapies that are available to us. When you play or coach sports, you must be in the present moment. This is wonderful for releasing trauma or negative mindsets. It also releases those feel-good hormones to help change your outlook.

If you are feeling stuck and would like to improve your life, the first step is to understand that good things are waiting for you. Trust that they will unfold.

ISABELLE AUBÉ

Isabelle Aubé is a certified lifestyle coach specialising in helping women overcome past trauma and move into a more fulfilling and abundant space. She is also a high performance futsal coach and head coach of Elite Futsal Canada.

Isabelle was a 2020 Global Top 500 Award recipient, among esteemed individuals such as Elon Musk, Jim Kwik, Kamala Harris, and Greta Thunberg, for her contributions in the Sports Industry and Indigeneous communities.

She balances her time creating powerful shifts for her clients and preparing futsal athletes for international competitions, as Canada Women's Futsal National Team Manager for the Canadian National Futsal Association.

INVITATION FROM THE AUTHOR

If you are interested in a personal tarot reading, I would like to invite you to book in for a session (donation based) with me here:

https://bit.ly/2Ue64Lc

CONNECT WITH THE AUTHOR

Business Name: Native Way Coaching Services
Website: www.nativewaycoachingservices.com
Facebook: www.facebook.com/nativewaycoachingservices
Email: i.aube.professional@gmail.com

Be true to yourself. Be your number one fan and celebrate all your wins!

Gabriela Stan

It's 2005. I am pregnant with our first baby, and my husband and I are buying a business, a childcare center nearby. I have been wanting to start a business for a while and this business venture seems attractive; there is demand for more local childcare centers, and I believe it would be a good niche to get into. I am keen to get this project rolling before the baby is born.

I spend hours talking with the relevant compliance bodies, and I'm on site to ensure various required inspections meet the standards. But then, we find out that the seller has not been telling us the truth. We have been misled with vital information about enrollment numbers, and the accuracy of the accounting raises big question marks. When this is revealed to me, I hear my heart begin thumping. My stress levels hit the roof. We are already too far into the deal to back out now.

I'm embarrassed when I realize that we've used the same solicitor as the seller. Rookie mistake. My lack of experience in business shows, and the fear sets in. We have a huge mortgage, my husband's new business and a baby on the way. Getting out of this deal will not be easy, especially since we are collaborating with the same solicitor as the seller. Although it's a clear conflict of interest, the solicitor reassures us that "it should be okay". However, as the issues start to surface, things are not okay. The battle has begun, and I need to convince another solicitor to take over the case and get me out of the mess. Working against the clock, I call every law company in the area and explain our situation.

After numerous calls and countless rejections, I finally come across a mad lawyer! He likes the drama and I am in the middle of it.

We are able to back out of the deal after spending significant money and are now living on one income. For a while I can enjoy being a new mum. I take my daughter out on long strolls. I love not having to rush to be at work and leave her behind. I'm present for every milestone in her development. It's a beautiful rest from the rat race; however this break does not last as long as I intended. Reality sets in. My family depends upon a second income, and I return to work with dark circles under my eyes, and a sensitive body still recovering from a C-section just seven weeks prior. The two hour drive each way to work begins to tear me apart. It's just more time away from my baby, and I wonder what I'm missing out on as I sit in traffic.

One late afternoon in October, after coming home tired and stressed, I get the best phone call. I receive an offer for a job that's only fifteen minutes from home! This is a great opportunity to work in a prestigious dental practice. As a dental clinician I am excited to share my knowledge and skills in my local community. Things are starting to look great and the time I used to spend in traffic is now spent at home with my family.

It's now 2009. Our second daughter is born and I am working four jobs as well as running my own business. During the day I work at two dental clinics, and at night I teach at two different course levels, one of which runs at night. Mondays are my dreaded days: I leave at 7 a.m. and don't get back home until 10 p.m. Simultaneously, I'm running my own health awareness and promotion business. I run sessions any time I can: evenings, weekends, school holidays, you name it. It's never a dull moment here. Work is secure and comfortable, but I am not settled. I find my imagination drifting as I sit in my office, as I play with my daughters. My desire to formulate a new business plan increases with every passing day.

One day, a strong idea pops into my head and I launch into research mode. I have been thinking about the childcare center business model; I have never given up on it and I know it would work, but finding an affordable one is proving super hard. So I shift my thinking and the answer pops into my head:

A children's play center.

Different business model but still in demand and trending at present.

I quickly find a business for sale: a children's playland with a café in a major shopping center. I can picture new things for this already happy place. I envisage a vibrant atmosphere with lots of laughing children. A bouncing castle with obstacles and a slide landing in hundreds of colorful balls!

Sounds like fun, right? At coffee one day, as I told her about my new venture, my girlfriend laughed and said, "Most parents buy a swing set or a trampoline for their kids, but you buy the whole play center!"

Crazy, I know. We check the numbers with our accountant, and we get the green light. The offer is accepted and my mind gets to work. I want to create a space where parents can have time out while children have fun. I want to introduce different themes that cater for older children. We hold disco nights, themed parties, mascot naming competitions.

We introduce our center to occupational therapy groups to be used as a gym. The cafe is used for children's parties and christenings.

I have this vision, and two kids and four jobs do not stop me from pursuing it. It might seem like enough for a person to handle, but I'm at the point in my career where I need to try something different, to address this deep wish. I desire something that could produce a passive income for me and my family. My profession has certain limitations, and I long for flexibility and an alternative to trading my time for money. I strive for financial freedom, to be able to afford to do things we enjoy.

I spend every spare minute marketing, creating events, and reviewing the business model to grow this play center to its full potential. I work at the center at night, and work at my other jobs during the day. I power through my sleep deprivation to brainstorm innovative ways to help the play center succeed. Then, during breaks at my day job, I call suppliers, order stock, book clients and agents, and more.

I hire staff and spend endless hours training them. Then I realize I am spending every spare dollar on this business. We have not taken a paycheck for ourselves. This doesn't bother me yet. I knew this would not be an easy ride. A new business requires sacrifices and I'm not scared of the hard work. My commute is forty-five minutes, and I arrive after hours to clean, perform maintenance, and bring in supplies. We begin sacrificing family time to completely invest ourselves in the business. After working double shifts at work, we drive with two kids to the play center. It's dark, it's cold and instead of enjoying family time, we put ourselves out there to get this working.

While we are aware that the shopping center's complex and harsh rules will affect our business, we endure. They are stringent with access to the center. Any repairs are to be completed by their contractors, and the premises are regularly inspected to meet guidelines.

And, too soon, the day has come when our business is no longer viable. We have overstretched all our resources, and with people being money-conscious due to the global financial crisis, they aren't spending money to bring their children to our play center. I have failed, again. I can no longer afford the exuberant rent fees, the bills, and the staffing. The business is costing more than it is making. The only way out is to sell or surrender the lease.

But who wants to buy a children's play center during a global financial crisis? In addition, center management has no interest in finding another tenant because they are still getting paid. Every day grows harder, as we don't know who to pay first.

It's 2013. After six months of financial hardship, a client agrees to buy the business at a loss. At this point, I am prepared to take anything and grateful that someone has shown interest. Every day suspense grips me as I wait for the exchange to happen.

And finally, the day comes where we no longer own the business. A massive weight lifts off my shoulders, and we dive back into our normal lives. No more driving for hours after work, no more late nights, no more coffees to make, no more kids screaming, and no more plastic balls to wash! We can now enjoy weekends and nights with our children. We can live life and do things we enjoy, no longer tied to the demanding business.

But what else is there to worry about? Well, we still have a business loan. So our struggles do not relent. I work harder than ever in my job to repay the monthly loan. In truth, everything is not suddenly better after selling our business. But we persist, we console each other, and we do not let this battle conquer us.

I am not angry, upset, or disappointed. I know I gave the business all I could. I tried all the possible avenues I could imagine at the time. Looking back, I see the shortcomings and gaps in my skill and knowledge. While it's true that I was focused and determined, I know I lacked experience. On this point I was stubborn, thinking I could do it all on my own. I didn't understand when it was time to ask for help, even though I so badly wanted to succeed.

These thoughts haunt me, and shame invades the very core of who I am. I am a failure. I feel helpless and frustrated thinking about the effort that was put into this venture with little success. My body is feeling the strain of insomnia and headaches become a regular symptom. What could have been done differently? What did I miss? I realize I can't just sit here and feel sorry for myself. The business loan must be paid. I need answers to the questions lingering in my head. I need closure. This frustration pushes me to look for more options.

So, I launch into research mode. I embrace my shortcomings and become a student again. I read books and magazines, listen to podcasts, and attend business workshops. At a business workshop in Sydney at one of the major hotels, in a conference room full of people, the presenter talks about business stages, success and how to prevent failures. Here, I finally discover where I went wrong. I recognize and admit that my failure may be linked to a lack of mentorship. I did not reach out to people, the right people. Having a mentor and the right team to guide and support you is a must.

It's been five years since I sold my business. I dust myself off and go again. With the world changing and consumer habits leaning towards online shopping, it makes sense to be part of this "space". The borderless shopping experience and internationalization of consumers. I believe it's the right time to be associated with such a business. So, I make it my goal and project to embark on the import/export and e-commerce journey.

This online project is complex, exciting, and frightening at the same time. The online world is much more involved than most people realize. Sourcing products from overseas suppliers takes this business to another level. I possess little IT knowledge, yet here I am, embarking on this task!

However, I have a different perspective now. I have the right support and mentors, and I am following a formula that has brought and keeps bringing success to a lot of people. I have joined a community that communicates well and shares expertise. Being able to work from any location sounds very attractive; getting away from being trapped between four walls is appealing. Although, there are challenges as with any other job or business. I must perform project management via long distance. Not as easy as it sounds!

There are days when I ask myself why I pursue business. E-commerce promises work under pressure, which is what I thrive at, but it is my "why" that gives me that extra strength and determination. I still chase the same end goal: financial freedom that would allow us to live and experience life! There are so many more things to tick off the bucket list.

In this business I tackle new and exciting challenges: language barriers, different cultural standards, and different time zones; the list goes on! Something important to remember is to never assume people understand my intentions, my vision and to never assume I fully understand theirs. People have different standards of what they expect in terms of loyalty and quality.

Having a business is not "a side hustle"! There are long nights, stressful situations and times when I make choices that affect family life. But it's no worse than if I worked overtime in a job far away from home, making someone else money. Things aren't always falling right into place, but I am much more prepared this time.

This business brings out the "BOSS" in me. I stand strong and stick to my word. I will not let anyone push me over anymore! In addition, the mentors' support gives me clarity and drives me to keep going. There are always hurdles and hiccups. The constant reinforcement and guidance are what I needed all along. Technology is making mentor accessibility and continual engagement easier.

Sometimes, memories of my failed business ventures impact my decision-making. I fear taking risks and procrastinate because of it. I am not as spontaneous as I used to be. I know what my goal is; I need to scale the business to the next level. But for some reason, the "what ifs" still prowl around. Fear of the unknown is not easy to overcome. Fear of losing the "security" of a job is holding me back and affects my ability to grow my business.

Being well aware of my doubts, I can commit to investing time and effort into changing this fear of failure. I invest in myself and ensure I am present, putting myself in the room with those who can give me the direction and skills to overcome any concerns and fears. Fear, patience, persistence, determination, resilience, and tenacity are all things I have exercised over the past fifteen years. The combination of these helps me stay focused and propels me towards my goals. Nothing beats the feeling of achieving a long-term goal.

The day when I pay off my business loan finally comes, and it is such a relief! We do not make a fuss, but the easement of stress is welcomed. Reflecting on the past few years, it was hard, testing, and stressful, but it made me stronger and more able to face what is yet to come.

I can now spend more time with my family and more time building my new business. My husband and I work hard, and family time is precious. We travel and explore. We can now take time out and make some more memories.

Business wise, I play the long game, taking my time to get this right and not repeat the same mistakes. I am now realigned, ready to overcome any obstacles. Sure, there are detours, but nothing blocks my path. I am anchored, and I am surrounding myself with great, like-minded people and connections. Mentors are a must; this cannot be understated.

• • •

You must walk the walk to experience it, but having support along the way makes the walk more balanced and pleasant. The bumps in my journey did not change the direction or destination, they only delayed the arrival. Although there is so much more to do and strive for, I am glad I have embarked on this journey, and I am proud to say that I have an Australian business with a trademarked brand that sells products online across the world!

How amazing is that? I am proud that I have not given up when times have been tough, and that my business can reach people near and far. Every win, no matter how large or small, needs to be celebrated. Stay focused and push hard. The fighting spirit needs to be brought out and if it's not there, find it!

Don't do this alone. There is help and guidance out there, you just need to find what works for you. Joining people with similar goals and ambitions, as well as having knowledgeable and passionate mentors, gets you to the wins or "endgame" as some of my mentors call it! Stretch the mind and expand the imagination. You'll be surprised where it takes you.

GABRIELA STAN

Gabriela Stan is the founder of Marliz, an online homewares store that sources beautiful products made for comfortable living.

Gabriela is also a seasoned educator, clinician, mentor, and dental consultant. She holds a Masters of Education and runs a health promotion and dental consultancy business.

Her dental experience spans over twenty-five years, and she uses her wealth of knowledge to help her clients make healthy choices, with a special focus on oral health and overall health.

INVITATION FROM THE AUTHOR

Let us help you add a personal touch and sense of comfort to your home!
Visit our shop Marliz to explore our range of unique homewares.

CONNECT WITH THE AUTHOR

Business Name: Marliz
Website: www.marliz.com.au
Email address: admin@marliz.com.au

*The key to success
is to recognize that
change is inevitable.*

Khemara Sical

Boston looks amazing in the evening. There is less bustle on the streets. I can't hear the cars honking their horns, or the sound of construction that took place earlier in the day.

I'm standing in my office, looking out of the floor to ceiling windows into the city lights. I've just found a moment of peace in my day, as I sip my passion fruit tea from one of my coffee mugs.

I hear the vacuum going on just cubicles away, and the voices of the cleaning crew, discussing whether the floors were done. They come every day after the building shuts down at 7:00 p.m. I look at the time on my monitor and see it's getting close to 8:30 p.m. and remember I have to text my husband to let him know I won't be home for dinner again tonight. He texts back, "Try to get home soon, if you can!"

A few minutes later I hear a text message notification on my phone. It's my daughter. We were supposed to make cookies tonight for her school tomorrow. I promised I'd take her shopping to get the ingredients. I responded to her text, "Can you ask your dad to take you?"

She replies, "But, Mom, you promised."

I text back, "Ok, I'll be home in a few, just make sure you're ready."

I look at the screen of my dual monitors and see meeting after meeting booked on my calendar for tomorrow. Another busy day, I think to myself. I try to squeeze in time on my calendar to work on the many projects I have on my plate. I book off my lunch time and think to myself, ten minutes for lunch is plenty.

• • •

Back in 2018, this was an average day in my life. My workload was high, forcing me to work overtime on most evenings. I was trying to be everything to everyone. I truly felt like I had lost control and couldn't say no to anything that was asked of me.

I was experiencing complete burnout, yet I tried to convince myself that this was what success was supposed to look like; that achieving more meant working more. I told myself I had the bandwidth to get every-thing done by the deadline. I told myself that the money was worth it.

At night, I couldn't sleep. I kept wondering if I had forgotten some-thing that I had to do at home or at work. When I did sleep, I had nightmares and would dream about things that just didn't make sense. In one such recurring dream, I'd walk into the office with nothing on other than my black leather stiletto heel pumps and matching black leather tote bag. My colleagues and boss would greet me with a "Good morning," as they looked down at my exposed body. I would cringe but still stand there, letting them look at me. I'd then scurry along to sit at my desk and log into my desktop, feeling mortified.

During the day I would become irritated and frustrated at the slightest things. I'd yell at my husband for leaving his socks on the sofa, and snap at my daughter when she made a comment about something I'd forgotten. Most days I just thought to myself, is this really it?

At home, things were just as overwhelming.

My son had just turned one and was adapting to some new changes in his schedule, so he was fussy most of the time. My son was very colicky which meant we had many sleepless nights. My husband and I would take turns to get up to feed him and rock him back to sleep, sometimes until four in the morning.

I was working sixty-plus-hour work weeks, all while launching two businesses. One of the businesses was a medical supply company. I had worked diligently on launching a product that acted like second skin to advance the healing of wounds for patients suffering from diabetes. I was passionate about the business, but sometimes it felt like just another drain on my time.

My daughter had started a new school and was struggling with her grades. I thought that if she knew how hard her mother worked, that it would inspire her to do well.

I was struggling to be there for her, to help her through all her school work, or even to give her some motivation. When I got home from work, I would eat dinner then disappear into my office to finish up my tasks. I would work well into the late hours of the evening.

One evening, I was sitting at dinner with my daughter. I watched her across the table. She was on her phone, texting her friend. I realized that she'd grown up so much. She wasn't the little girl I once knew. I started to recall the times when she was younger, when all her attention was on me. She used to love watching me get dressed up.

"Mom, when will I be able to wear a dress like that?" my daughter, who was seven at the time, asked as she watched me standing in front of the mirror.

I replied to her, "When you're forty-five, darling."

She responded, "But, Mom, you're not forty-five!"

I couldn't help but giggled at her response.

After that day, she would go into my closet and admire my clothes. This was not the first or only time my daughter would observe my actions. She questioned everything she saw her mother do or take an interest in. As a mother with a daughter, I always felt that my happiness was crucial to her success in life. I wanted to see her grow up to become a strong woman. More than anything, I wanted to see her happy.

My daughter's voice shook me out of my reverie. She had asked me what was wrong, and I realized I was crying, silent tears spilling onto the kitchen table. I confessed to her that I wanted her to see me as a role model for herself, because, growing up, that was something I always lacked. My daughter then spoke the words that I will never forget: "It's not your success that makes us happy, it's when you're happy, that makes us happy."

They were simple words, but they had such a profound effect on me. Her insight shifted the way I saw success for myself. That's how my passion for helping others find their own fulfillment in all aspects of their lives really began. I wanted to inspire my daughter to stand up in a way that was empowering for her. I wanted her to unapologetically take a stand for the things that made her happy.

Our passion has the power to change the world. But if you want change, it has to start from you. For me it started within the home, with my daughter. Because I wanted better for my children, I wanted better for myself.

As women, we're taught to put others first. And when we're asked the question, "What is it that you desire?" it's never easy to admit that we want something for ourselves.

But when the question is asked with those we love in mind, "What is it that you desire for your children?" the response becomes easy.

• • •

I look at the clock in my home office and it has just struck 11:00 p.m. My eyes, still red from staring at my screen all day, are dry and itchy and I can feel them slowly wanting to shut off. I look over to the luggage that's supposed to be packed for my trip to Miami, Florida. My flight leaves at 3:30 p.m. tomorrow and all I can think about is getting this report out for work.

Thirty minutes later I finally hit the send button on my email. I let out a sigh of relief as now I can think about my much needed vacation. I'm picturing myself laying on a beach with my large brim beach hat and oversized sunglasses as I sip fruity pink cocktails. This is what I work so hard for, I think to myself.

As I'm brushing my teeth getting ready for bed I hear a notification on my phone. It's a reply email from my colleague asking to speak to me tomorrow morning at 7:00 a.m. I responded with "OK" and accepted the meeting invitation. I think to myself, it will probably be a quick touch-base and I will pack after our call, but right now it's already midnight and I just need to get to bed.

That night, the same nightmare of me exposed and naked at work happens again. But this time, everyone is standing around me and whispering words that I can't understand. I am the center of attention, still nude with just my shoes and handbag. I hunch down into a ball to try to hide myself, but there is nowhere to hide. My alarm clock rings and I wake up feeling uneasy, but tell myself that it was just a dream.

I take the call with my colleague and he asks for the revisions on my report, just five hours before I have to leave for my flight. My suitcases are still unpacked and I am nowhere near ready for my trip. I tell him I am leaving for a trip and I can't get it out this morning, but he insists that he needs it by tomorrow morning because of a big meeting he has to attend. I promise him I will send him the revisions this evening when I land.

I didn't plan on bringing my laptop with me, but here I am, forty thousand feet high, typing away, revising a report to send out to my colleague. I send it right before I land in Miami. Finally, time to relax.

• • •

I knew what I had to do. I blocked out the next three months to plan my departure from corporate and muster up the courage to hand in my notice.

On the first day of this master plan I was standing in the bathroom in front of the mirror. I looked down at my stomach and felt the softness of it. I felt so out of shape after giving birth to my son. Before he was born I remember being in one of the best shapes of my life. I wondered what it would be like to feel confident and in shape again.

I began taking boxing classes in the evenings after work, and I hired a personal trainer on the weekends. While I was face to face with the punching bag, hitting it with all my strength, I felt a sense of release. All of this built-up energy just came out. My trainer gave me the nickname, "Killer K". Week by week, I began to see how my body had changed. I was standing stronger and feeling more confident. I was seeing muscles in places they'd never existed before. I also worked on de-stressing through meditation. I dedicated forty-five minutes in the evening to a meditation routine, and in the mornings, I would say positive affirmations. I also began to balance my time better, saying no to things that were just not a priority for me. Before I knew it, I was building up my mind, body, and spirit in preparation for the exit.

It was the morning of April 15. I had written up my resignation notice. For a moment I almost backed out. I had built up a much better balance for myself within the past three months, and I thought maybe I could sustain it. Then I heard a voice that just said, "Do it!" That's it, I thought to myself, there is no turning back.

At the meeting my boss and I discussed reports and anything else that I had on my plate. We discussed some upcoming deadlines and meetings. Then I told her that I had something else I would like to discuss with her.

"This was not an easy decision," I said as I handed her the resignation notice.

"We'll take care of everything on this end," she said as she took my letter. She didn't seem surprised at all.

The next morning, I got an email from her. She offered me a counter-offer to stay. A part of me knew that the money would be great, but I told her that I really needed to leave because no amount of money was worth my wellbeing.

I was able to take a year off for my personal development. I embarked on a journey that led me to embrace deep inner work through meditations and mindfulness techniques. This brought me back to being present and learning how to manage my feelings so that I could continue to thrive in my business and be fully present for my family. Leaving my job was difficult. The decision to start my own business was not. Leaving my job had nothing to do with money, and everything to do with my choice to prioritize my life and the things I valued most.

I'd always wanted to help people improve themselves. But this was my opportunity to help myself first, so I could go on to help others. This was my opportunity to serve. I enrolled in a coaching program, and even took on clients before I was certified. As my coaching business grew, I realized there was an opportunity here to provide tools and resources to people to help them improve their lives through meditation and mindfulness. I knew first hand the benefits of slowing down, being more mindful, and being open to change.

Running my own business gave me clarity about who I wanted to be: someone who stayed passionate about doing something they loved, but not someone who sacrificed everything to get there. Taking this step is hard. It's scary and difficult. You might feel like you've made a mistake or that life has changed too drastically. But making this change requires perseverance and focus as well as bravery and faith.

If you find yourself in the same situation I was in, remember, no matter what your reasons for changing your life, or how difficult it is, there are things you can learn from it. Leading a new business and loving it while it's growing is hard work. The good news is that once you get your head around running a startup, and are committed to making real progress towards your goals, the struggles are much less daunting.

• • •

We've become very good at holding onto stress, negative emotions, unconscious blocks and patterns that have taken control of our life. Prioritizing yourself is difficult when you are working and taking care of everyone and everything else. One of the most important things you can do is to make time for yourself, even if it is for five minutes a day to set the intention that this time is for you. Use this time to do things that you enjoy, whether that is having a cup of tea, meditating, writing in your journal or simply shutting your eyes. Once you have a routine where the intention is placed on yourself, gradually build up to making more time for yourself.

I've found that there is so much more peace in my home life now. My son is sleeping better and is less fussy. My daughter is doing exceptionally well at school. She even brags about having the highest score in one of her classes. I'm able to cook and be home for almost every single dinner with my family.

I no longer feel the pressure to fulfill my duties at home by working 60 hour weeks. I am more able to spend time with friends and family. Leaving my corporate job has freed up my time to do something I've always dreamed of, on my own terms. Being in this position has also made me realize how fortunate I really am to have access to some of the best tools and wellness resources out there. I no longer believe that having a job is the be-all and end-all. There is much more to life than working a nine-to-five job that no longer excites you.

The recurring nightmares have stopped and I sleep soundly at night, knowing that I am able to make an impact in my home life, while making an impact in other people's lives. Running a coaching business has its challenges. Yet, it has been incredibly rewarding. The success I have seen so far has made me realize something: If I remain passionate about what I do, I can create great change in my life—even if it's only in the here and now.

KHEMARA SICAL

Khemara Sical is a transformational life coach, and meditation teacher based in Boston, MA. In a world where navigating our well-being is challenging, her work takes into consideration the interconnectedness of her client's mind, body, and spirit to ensure sustainable transformation from the inside and out.

Her unique coaching framework is based on the premise that when you reconnect to and embrace your totality, you position yourself to thrive in any aspect of your life. Khemara has a proven process to affect change even in the most challenging times.

In 2013 Khemara suffered a severe mechanical back injury that left her in tremendous pain, unable to walk or stand. It was there, at the base of the spine—the sacrum—that triggered the entire awakening process. She began teaching herself how to self-heal through the power of meditation and mindfulness, and has seen the abundant effects of it unfolding in different aspects of her life.

Khemara then spent years learning about meditation and holistic healing techniques and went on to become a certified meditation teacher, certified corporate wellness coach, and certified holistic life coach. She also has extensive training in mindfulness-based stress reduction, breathwork, hypnotherapy, chakra and aura healing, and Ayurveda. She is passionate about teaching people how to harness their limitless potential through meditation and wellness tools.

INVITATION FROM THE AUTHOR

Schedule your FREE introductory consultation to see how I can help you create the blueprint for your success!

http://bit.ly/intro_ks

CONNECT WITH THE AUTHOR

Business Name: Empowered Life Wellness
Website: www.facebook.com/empoweredlifewellness.co
Facebook: www.facebook.com/khemarasicalofficial
Email: hello@empoweredlifewellness.co

We are Source made manifest; thoughts that think for the growth and expansion of our collective consciousness.

Deb Norman

Have you ever sat under the sky at night and watched the stars glisten and move, wondering if there is more to your existence?

I have spent years sitting under the stars, contemplating who and what I am versus who and what I was led to believe I am. As a child, I remember feeling this urgent unwavering need to connect to my origin on this planet, however, it never really felt like home here on earth. There was always that sense of déjà vu, entangled with glimpses of other life experiences in other places. I had no awareness at the time that these feelings were activated in my DNA, or that this process was affected by the planetary line up, designed to assist me in my earthly experience. My body's genetic codes are layered with lifetimes of lessons I have learned, knowledge I have accumulated, and experiences I have encountered, all of which nudge me to use my gifts to serve the collective.

I now understand what the purpose of this incarnation is and know that we are different expressions of the one vibration looking to experience itself.

• • •

Being born with psychic abilities means never being alone, not even in the bathroom. As a six-year-old I remember running down the hall in the middle of the night in total terror as I watched the shadows follow me. They were Victorian era women standing in the doorway of my bathroom, with umbrellas over their heads, staring at me as if in astonishment at my presence. I was so scared that I tried to punch one and it was like there was an invisible force field preventing contact. I screamed and ran away, while my mother said dismissively, "There goes Deb again." She had no understanding of the trauma I was experiencing. For someone who was never alone, I felt so alone. This was what set the foundation for the rest of my early life; a foundation based on an unsupportive family system that led to my feelings of isolation, abandonment, and fear that filled every cell in my body. Little did I know back then, that by changing one simple thought pattern, I could change my world.

Up until a child is seven years old, their brainwaves are in what is called a theta state. What this means is that they are absorbing one hundred percent of everything they see, feel, and hear within their surroundings. Within the first week of kindergarten, I was ridiculed by the teacher in front of the whole class for putting a lead pencil in my mouth. She asked me every minute for an hour whether I was dead yet. By second grade I had managed to get myself locked in a storeroom by a teacher, belittled daily for talking out of turn—belted, bullied, and abused by those who I trusted to care for me.

In this way, life tried to break me. I withdrew more and more, holding out hope that another teacher, my father, someone, would rescue me. This is when my program was born. The program that I then took out into the world, looking to be saved by a knight in shining armor. And of course, we all know how that fairy-tale ends.

• • •

It was just after my eighteenth birthday that I got married and fell pregnant with twins. I could not believe my luck. My knight had arrived, and, in my mind, he would save me from the despair and rejection I had experienced with my family. Finally, I would escape the craziness. I had married a man who loved me. We had babies on the way. Everything was going to be ok. Or was it?

Married life was hard. I was young and unaware of what to expect or how to act as no one had prepared me. My husband was in his twenties when we got married. He drove a cool car, he had tattoos all down his arms, and curly blonde hair down to his shoulders. He was a rebel. At first, I felt swept away by his raw, unwavering attitude, but as a wife and mother it became harder to manage emotionally. He would go missing for days on alcohol and drug benders, leaving me to run the home, get up constantly to two screaming babies, all without a car, support, or money. It is obvious to me now that he did not want to be in the marriage, that he felt trapped. Back then I was unable to see this. No matter how bad it got, I believed that this was normal and a part of being married, as I had learned from a young age that men abandon the women in their lives—this had played out in my early environment with my parents. I was in such denial about the abuse, rejection, loneliness, and betrayal.

I convinced myself that I was loved and that I had a purpose. After all, this was what I was groomed for. My role was to look after everyone else, make them happy, ensure they were cared for at the expense of myself. This was what a good wife and mother did. I thought if I loved more, did more, I would be loved in return.

My parents tried to tell me that my situation was not healthy, yet at the same time they told me that I had made my bed and now I had to lie in it. I found this contradiction extremely confusing. I started to lose my mind. I was exhausted, sick, and alone.

I fell into unhealthy eating patterns in an attempt to please him. The constant reinforcement that I was "fat" began to eat at me. I worked out at least three hours a day attempting to decrease my already petite size ten. What I did not realize then, is that I was beautiful. Why did I let others tell me I was fat and ugly? Why did I buy into it?

Life seemed to get harder over the next few years. My environment was chaotic. I was now twenty-two with another child. All I did was cook, clean, and attend to the children. I was consumed with old feelings of rejection again as my husband became more distant, rolling in drunk at all hours and forgetting where he was, and that was on the days that he came home.

My psychic ability was in overdrive. I would walk around the house for hours, making myself insane—I could see the paths laid out in front of me, the choices and roads always dictated by my husband. I could see his choices before he made them. I couldn't cope with what I was seeing, hearing, and feeling, yet I still had this insatiable urge to love him more with the delusion that I could fix or save him, and that he would love me for it.

One night, one of the twins had a severe asthma attack. I called my husband's workplace and asked for him, but they insisted that he had already left and was on his way. I knew they were lying for him. I begged them to put him on; I told them his daughter was having a severe attack and I had no help with the other children. I knew we would have to go to the hospital. I called a neighbor, and they looked after the children while we went to the hospital.

My husband never came home that night or the next. I had no choice but to call his father and brother and ask for help. My daughter spent five nights in an oxygen tent. It was on the third night that my husband's father and brother found him at a drug house out of his mind.

I wanted to leave him, but I had nowhere to go and was so scared. A part of me wanted to forgive him and be loved no matter what the cost. This was an early childhood conditioned response. I'd watched my mother do the same. It was programmed into me and I had no awareness of it at the time.

Before I knew it, I was twenty-three and pregnant again. But this one felt different. At twelve weeks I went for an ultrasound. I was having triplets. At thirteen weeks I was called in for another scan. This time a specialist was brought in. Two of the triplets were suffering: one had stopped growing and the other had a very faint heartbeat. The specialist told me I would lose all three, and shortly after the scan, two of them passed, pushing me into despair. It was a miracle that the third baby lived and was carried to full term. On my twenty-fourth birthday I went into labor which lasted three days. The baby was drowning and I was not doing well either. By the time the specialist got to me it was too late to do an emergency C-section. Both me and the baby nearly lost our lives. He was born with brain issues due to the lack of oxygen.

I was sick for a long time after the birth. My body had absorbed too many toxins and chronic fatigue had set in. This put a huge strain on an already broken relationship. I remember coming home five days after the labor to a week's worth of dishes and washing. My husband took off as soon as we got home, leaving me with the mess, three children under five, and a new baby. I felt broken.

My parents suggested moving to the country; the fresh air would help us come together, they said. Somehow, I managed to convince my husband. We put the house on the market and moved to the country where we stayed in a granny flat on my parents' property. Only when I got there did I realize that their motive was for me to help with the farm, not for them to help with the children. Once we arrived it was not long before we were not allowed in the house; my mother did not want them or me in there. So, we purchased a block of land 36 km out of town and pitched a tent.

I, my husband, and children all lived in a tent for four years while we built our own kit home on the thirty-acre property. There were no facilities; I collected wood and cooked on an open fire. One thing my childhood had taught me growing up on a farm was how to be resilient. I bathed the children in water I collected from the tanks at the back of our block. I hand washed dishes and clothes in old concrete tubs while waiting patiently for my husband to come back with food for dinner if we were lucky. Many times, we had little to eat.

I soon realized that things had to change. Once the house was built we moved the children back to the city and rented it out. It took five years to sell. Now that I was back in civilization, I could work on my health and look for a home for us.

I found a lovely spot on the central coast. We purchased a property with the money from the sale and renovated the house. I started training in nursing and was feeling positive about the new start. Then the behavior started again—drinking and driving, taking drugs, and not coming home. There had been other women in the past. Was he doing it again? It's getting out of control, I thought to myself, surely this is not how life is meant to be.

Then, in November 1995, I injured my back badly. After an eight-hour nursing shift of constant heavy lifting I was in excruciating pain. For the next two years I was in a rehab program of water aerobics and osteopaths as I could hardly walk or move, let alone go to work.

Soon, my worst fears were realized. It was going to take two years of fighting the insurance company to compensate for my injury, and I had a mortgage to pay. I was a casual, therefore only entitled to part pay for six months. I could not maintain the mortgage so the bank stepped in and within a month the house was gone. All was lost. I had failed; without a home, I was nothing.

Once I was stable and able to travel, we moved to the Gold Coast, but life did not improve as I hoped. I knew something had to change, so I sought support from others. I found two amazing mentors who I spent the next four years with. They taught me what I hadn't understood about myself, my predicament, my early conditioning, dramas, and everything that was creating what I did not want in my life. I did my training in spiritual awareness and development, and psychological astrology. These were some of the best years of my life. My focus was on the children, my own growth and happiness.

After many attempts to rebuild a marriage that was broken from the start, I decided to make a bold move and take the children and myself out of our unhealthy situation. My mentors never told me to leave. They focused on supporting my understanding and growth, which brought me to the point of seeing things the way they really were. It took another two years for me to break away from him, as the resistance and fear felt overwhelming. How would I manage on my own? How would it affect the children? Going into the unknown paralyzed me with fear. I took a deep breath, built up the courage and did it; it was one of the hardest things I had ever had to do. I could feel my inner sabotage attempting to pull me back into the old way of thinking and being.

After a year of struggle, I managed to find us a nice house. I was teaching astrology and looking for more work. This is when my real estate career started. Now money was coming in and my weight was back to where I wanted it. I felt good within myself and I was creating a social life again.

A year later, I met a man through a friend. He appeared to be everything I could ever want, the knight coming in to sweep me off my feet. He was tall, built like Vin Diesel. He would open the door for me. He wowed me with my first experience in an actual restaurant. My first husband never acknowledged an anniversary or my birthday or Christmas.

My career was doing well. I was selling two properties a week and studying to be a principal. Then the unthinkable happened. One morning, after getting the kids to school and rushing to work, I became nauseas. I raced to the doctors in my lunch hour. I waited, dreading the results.

"Congratulations," the doctor said. "You're pregnant."

I imagined his reaction; I had the worst feeling of dread in the pit of my stomach. That night I met him for dinner. The air felt thick. It was as if he knew something was up. Finally, I blurted out the truth. It felt like the earth stopped moving. The silence between us was deafening. He left our dinner to have a drink with his friend. It was the worst thing he could have done, but I let him go, and said nothing. The next day he informed me that he was being sent on a job interstate, and I knew that was his way of leaving. My son grew up without his dad. Those years were some of the hardest I had to face. My son was extremely sick, born with stomach issues.

My father gave me the money to see a specialist who sent tests to the States. Nothing could have prepared me for the results. The doctor pulled up the test results and told me my son was dying. He had multiple bacteria, one of which was killing him. His body was full of mold spores, inhaled from a rental property. And he had a tapeworm in his bile duct from a sheep farm we had stayed on. His medication and treatments were expensive. It was costing more than I could earn. I was on a pension and had exhausted all resources. We soon became homeless. This frightening experience lasted for a year.

How much pain does it take to get someone to move?

My father finally stepped in and helped us out financially. I got treatment for my son, a unit to rent, a computer to start studying again, and slowly but surely, I began to heal. I studied with some amazing mentors. Looking back now, it was these harsh times that challenged me to be better, look for answers, dive deep into my own psyche and master self-awareness. It took another seven years of study before I was able to align myself with the resources to build a home—somewhere we could feel safe, while my son healed, and I became more centered. I now take care of my father as I am forever grateful that he pulled me out of the well.

. . .

Years of reflection, study, and experiences have given me the ability to see programs and come up with strategies and solutions that reverse the trauma souls create without awareness. I feel so blessed to have had these experiences, as I am now able to help other women who have found themselves in similar situations break free of their genetic codes.

If only I had only known when I was young what I know now, what a different life experience I would have lived. But the way I see it, in the end, we create what we need to reach our deepest parts of self, to transcend our shadow into light, and expand on our ability to love and create more than we ever imagined.

DEB NORMAN

Deb Norman is the CEO of The Quantum Blueprint, an educational platform that supports clients and students in understanding their past pain points and how to release and replace these paradigms with thought patterns that nurture future growth.

Deb is qualified in psychological astrology and Jung based psychotherapy, energy body work, strategic coaching, spiritual awareness and personal development, Reiki, Secheim, Theta healing and metaphysics, and is currently studying with Dr Bruce Lipton in epigenetics.

Deb was born a psychic/medium. She studied for twenty-six years with experts in their field including Tony Robbins, Bob Proctor, Jeffrey Allen, Maggie Kerr and Dr. Bruce Lipton.

She was awarded VIP status for psychological astrology, and included in the book of Worldwide Who's Who for 2014 and 2015.

Deb's passion is educating people who feel stuck in the loop of their early family conditioning.

INVITATION FROM THE AUTHOR

You are not alone, and there is a solution to every challenge. I would love you to join our FREE group of 27,500+ other souls who come together to support one another and learn about themselves and their environment.

www.facebook.com/groups/1777610465870359/

CONNECT WITH THE AUTHOR

Business name: The Quantum Blueprint
Website: www.thequantumbp.com/
Facebook: www.facebook.com/quantumblueprint
Email: quantum.blueprint3@gmail.com

You are enough, and you don't have to prove that to anyone. You deserve to be successful and express who you are.

Danni Dandan Gadigan

I magine a movie opens on a scene in a suburban city in Buffalo, NY, and a young Asian American girl, Danni, is climbing the steep steel steps of the school bus.

"Your face looks like it was run over by a semi-truck," one of the rowdy twin boys from the back of the bus shouts, followed by laughter.

Embarrassed and taken by surprise, Danni laughs awkwardly and quickly sits in the front seat behind the bus driver, puts her gray and pink backpack on her knees, and sinks down low attempting to cover her face.

Cut to middle school, and Danni is desperately trying to be someone else. Her plan to make her eyes wider and to keep her jaw open while closing her mouth to make her face appear less Asian is brilliant. Her classmates wonder why she looks so shocked as she struts down a runway of lockers and students; but in her mind she is a whole new person, someone more beautiful and more worthy of love.

High school Danni struggles with bulimia and never feels good enough. She dates older guys that give her the attention she craves; but the relationships are toxic.

Watching this movie now, I wish I could hug that girl and tell her how she has always been beautiful and worthy of love and all good things. I'm sure you've figured out that that girl is me, and those were moments of my life story.

I used to think, if only I could go back in time knowing what I know now and make better decisions, I may have saved myself a lot of heartache. But, just like in a movie, each character has their own arc and their challenges are what shape them, making them stronger and more relatable. Plus, how boring would a movie be if the main character never had to navigate through tough times? It would rob them and the viewers of the bittersweet emotions that come with each win, and all the quirky characters that help them along the way would end up on the cutting room floor.

The wounds of other people's words cut deep, but what hurt me the most was how their opinions of me sneakily transformed into my opinions of myself. My inner critic hijacked my voice, and my mind, and would relentlessly regurgitate the insults. At that point, I didn't realize that I could make a daily conscious choice to be either my biggest bully and despised nemesis, or my biggest fan and compassionate companion.

Some of the most moving moments in our favorite movies are when the character takes a stand and finally changes what they are doing because they know they deserve better. I'm here to share some of the hardest moments in my life that were opportunities in disguise to "rise up"!

• • •

One question which terrified and plagued me throughout high school and college was this: What do you want to do with your life?

"My daughter got into Harvard, Yale, *and* Princeton."

"My son is valedictorian."

"My daughter is taking three AP classes this year, and five next year."

These were some of the conversations that my mom always seemed to stay quiet in. Every other parent had phenomenal things to share about their kids, and I desperately wanted my parents to have those talking points, too. What was wrong with me? Everyone around me seemed to be excelling and on the path to success, and I was a black sheep, a dummy amongst geniuses.

Perhaps it was a self-fulfilling prophecy, or rebellion, or lack of interest, but my grades suffered and it was hard to shake the bad-student label. I felt worthless and judged and I started to buy into the lies and labels myself. I became my own sadistic tormentor and I couldn't escape the cycle of nasty thoughts.

I wanted to disappear, and I felt like I wouldn't be missed. My grades had suffered in all areas but one; there was a spark of inspiration in my favorite class, art. This was my oasis, a place where I could express myself to the fullest. My mom had encouraged creativity since grade school, sending me to art classes, ballet classes, and piano classes, and all of it is embedded in who I am today.

I remember, every Sunday, she would drop me off at an art teacher's home which had the familiar smell of eggs and Chinese food. Her house was full of knickknacks and furniture, and it was warm and inviting. I loved sitting at the table with my fellow classmates once a week and practicing different techniques. We created art with oil pastels, colored pencils, charcoal, Chinese watercolor, and we even did Chinese calligraphy.

The hours between when my mom dropped me off and picked me up trickled away like Chinese ink slowly seeping into rice paper. Half gossip, half check-in, it was a memorable time of fellowship as we honed our skills in art. Our eccentric host would walk around the room leaning over our shoulders to guide us, and then we would repeat what we'd learnt and run with it.

Tiger fur: press hard at first then end in a gentle lift, repeating over and over until you've filled in the tiger's face with texture and color.

Through the years of honing my skills, art became the one subject that I excelled at in school. I was still unsure of what to do in the future because being an artist of any sort was out of the question; that was a path that you would consider only if you were crazy.

So, I chose a few majors that I thought would be viable and jumped from communications to English to chemistry to biology. I received my degree in biology, but my heart wasn't really in it. Serendipitously, in my last year of college, my close friend recommended that I take a voice, diction, and movement class because of how fun and easy it was. Curious and excited about the prospect of an easy A, I took his suggestion and found my voice in that class in the theatre department of Buffalo State.

In that dimly lit theatre classroom edged with empty bleachers, black walls, wooden scenery flats, and duvetyn curtains, it was the first time I felt at home in a college class. I fell in love with the energy of a community of eclectic artists, being able to find and use my real voice, and the thrill of being at home with performing yet nudged outside of my comfort zone. The wild expression of random guttural sounds that came out of me surprised even myself. I was tuning into my body through awareness, relaxation, and movement. I became those animals that I had sketched in my childhood. I was happy about the person that I was becoming, someone who was free and open to possibilities.

I tried out for the college production, Hair. I landed an ensemble role and got to run wild in song and dance on stage with a tribe of ambitious creatives. I was able to tell stories with my mind, body, and spirit, and that was the most moving artform I've ever experienced.

• • •

Fast forward to Danni seeking out every opportunity possible to feed her passion. She joins an acting class and starts going to casting calls.

She moves to NYC, auditions for theatre and film productions, finds representation, books a role in her first film, and finally gets her SAG (Screen Actors Guild) card. Crying big tears of joy, she finally feels validation for being good at something.

She follows each sign, instinct, and gut feeling. One open door leads to another and she makes the big move to LA. She is finally flying after a late start.

• • •

It was the most exhilarating thing in the world to be booked on a project, because it meant someone believed I was worthy of being chosen for those special roles. They loved and chose me; but I had yet to love and choose myself.

Acting is all about the number of auditions you get. It's about preparation, mindset, and confidence. And like entrepreneurship it's also about embracing who you truly are and knowing you're enough, which gives you strength and endurance to weather the storms. It's about knowing what you have to offer and showing the real you. That means embracing everything about yourself, the good, the bad, and the ugly scenes in your movie. Those embarrassing scenes from your past are just as important as the moments when you feel on top of the world. It's what fills a life with exciting colors of adventure. Everyone lives for the big wins and shining successes, but the quiet moments behind the scenes are just as important.

At that time, I fell into the trap of just trying to land the role. I was people-pleasing and plagued with doubt. Am I pretty enough? Did I say the right thing? What did they want me to do? Am I making the right character choices? Do I look younger than the woman who auditioned before me? These questions grew the seed of doubt into an overgrown garden and I lost sight of my passion for storytelling.

Everyone knows rejection is part of the job, but my mindset at the time was very fragile and any hint of rejection became another suitcase of invisible baggage that weighed me down. Putting on a show and trying to prove my worth was the norm. I was trying to be everything for everyone else and ignoring my own needs. I had a constant sinking feeling at the thought that I hadn't accomplished enough, and I beat myself down to zero self-esteem. I was angry at myself, an unhappy bag of nerves, bitter and jealous of other people's success and cringing at their social media posts. The tiny pilot light of my dream was fading away in the background.

I was in a dark place, but I knew there had to be more to life than chasing after each booking. I had met my now husband Jeff, an actor as well, on set in Santa Monica. The thing that stood out about Jeff was that he was just as passionate about his role in front of the camera as he was about filming from behind the scenes. He saw both roles as an opportunity to tell a great story. I met him at a difficult time in my life and he helped me rekindle my love for storytelling.

One night, Jeff and I were at a restaurant in Florida. The performer there was singing "This Little Light of Mine", and it lit a fire in me. She sang with all her heart and with the freedom of a dove. It was clear that she loved what she did no matter what kind of audience she had and was doing exactly what God had made her to do. Hearing her message, I decided I wanted to go to church and asked Jeff if he knew of one. It turned out his friend was opening a church in downtown LA, so we went, and the first message I heard floored me.

"It's not about you, but helping other people, and being an ambassador for Christ."

The sermon and the sound of the band's peaceful gospel music had tears flowing down my face uncontrollably. The words put me at peace and gave me the desire to be part of something bigger. I felt a tugging on my heart and God saying, "You were meant to be in the industry, but it's not just for your dream anymore. You will make a bigger impact with your gifts by helping others achieve their dreams."

Jeff and I then had a lot of late-night talks about our own dreams and fears. We prayed for our families, friends, and careers. Our soul searching led us to start a production company, AminoCat Entertainment. Our experience in film set the stage for us to start our own venture.

• • •

Cut to the humble beginnings of AminoCat entertainment: Danni and Jeff working long hours, wearing all the hats, arguing with each other as they clumsily navigate how to work as a team of two.

After the messy mixing of work and family life, they learn to set boundaries and their business starts to grow.

Talented and creative friends in the industry come to work alongside them; they believe in AminoCat's vision. Although weeks and even months of unseen work go into each production behind the scenes, their filming and prep days are sprinkled with play and laughter.

AminoCat is bigger than them, and they are so grateful that they get to play a role in someone's life by giving them a shot at their dream.

• • •

I'd like to rewind to a scene in my movie from before we started our production company when I had a special opportunity to present the weather in Beijing.

My mom had always been my biggest supporter, yet she would also feel the need to voice her concerns about my career choices. This caused a lot of conflict between us because I wanted her support to look a certain way. It wasn't until I realized that her support and love came in her own way that our relationship started to thrive.

During the grueling screen test for the weather position that went on for a month, my mom would patiently give feedback on my hand gestures, my posture, and my inflections while I practiced. She was my coach and my loyal audience member. We had taped a big map of China onto the large window of my parents seventeenth floor condo as our makeshift version of a studio greenscreen, framed by the view of Beijing's bustling apartment buildings. My dad got involved and would quiz me on the geography of China while we were eating.

Naturally, my mom was the first person I called after I landed the weather gig and we were overjoyed to tears. My parents were so proud of me and it was something special our family accomplished as a team. Our friends would tune in to watch me presenting the weather, a huge smile on my face. And even my grandma, who doesn't speak English, would watch me on TV. She would tell me she didn't understand a word I said, but that I did a great job and it made her happy.

The Chinese community I had grown up with were able to see me in a different light and it felt good to represent them as well. I never thought I would be a weather presenter, but if you follow your heart, your dreams, and do what God made you to do, you'd better believe that doors will open for you. But you may not know exactly which ones until you get there.

I then had the opportunity to speak to a group of twenty-five kids at an international school about being a weather presenter. Afterwards my heart was so full of love and joy. Acting had given me the courage along with the confidence to speak in front of others, and by following my heart and dreams I was able to encourage a group of amazing kids to do the same. In a "full-circle" moment, I felt like I was speaking to my younger self in that group of energetic kids full of potential. I was able to give them the encouragement that I had desired at that age, and I hoped it could influence them to love themselves and honor the dreams in their own hearts.

• • •

Danni types on her computer, tears in her eyes and on her lips, smiling at everything that led up to the amazing opportunity to write this segment in a book full of incredible women. The world hasn't always been kind to her, and it is not always kind to women. And that's why we need to be extra kind to ourselves. Our minds, our bodies, and our souls.

We are worthy of great things; it's our birthright. And many of us are conditioned to believe differently somewhere along the way. God has made us beautiful, at all stages and ages in life. I say this to you with love and compassion in my heart because we work hard, we love with all our hearts, and we give generously. The funny thing is that sometimes we give a little too much of ourselves and put everyone else first. We deserve to love ourselves and take care of our own needs. When we honor our desires, we can give more to others from an overflowing cup of inner abundance.

I once felt like a failure because of my perspective, but all along I have been breaking through my own barriers and succeeding. I step outside of my comfort zone every day, meet new artists from different walks of life, create art, follow my heart, and gain momentum in an industry that is hard to break into.

When I stop and close my eyes, put my hand on my heart, I'm so grateful to be me, and once again those happy tears start welling up in my eyes. I realize that while my success doesn't look like anyone else's, and never will, my success is my own, and no one other than myself could ever take that away from me. It's my unique film that I can rewatch and enjoy, cry and laugh along with until my last breath.

I was made to live out my dream while encouraging and empowering other women to live out theirs. Together we can make an impact on the generations to come. Will you join me in a moment of self-love and put your hand on your heart, breathe deep and soak these statements in?

You are enough and you don't have to prove that to anyone.

Listen to the quiet voice of truth; the loud nasty voice has to be loud because it's not real.

You deserve your own kindness, especially when others aren't gentle.

Your God-given dreams and talents are important.

Shine, love, laugh, cry, dance, move, create, without holding back, because the world needs your unique unfiltered beauty.

Your story deserves to be heard.

You are the heroine of your epic movie. You've lived a lifetime of amazing scenes, and some of your best moments are yet to come. You are the only one who has the ability to step into your role of a lifetime, so play it with all your heart. You don't even have to memorize any lines!

> *"Arise, shine; for thy light is come, and the glory of the LORD is risen upon thee."*
>
> — ISAIAH 60:1 KJV

DANNI DANDAN GADIGAN

Danni Dandan Gadigan is a producer, photographer, cinematographer, actress, and the co-founder of AminoCat Entertainment. Her production company helps individuals and businesses bring their dream vision to video. They craft commercials, documentaries and films in impactful ways that share the most valuable asset of all, our stories.

Danni has had the blessing of working on several TV shows, films, commercials, animated films, and soaps. With over fifteen years in the industry working with networks such as NBC, CBS, USA, and CCTV, both in front of and behind the camera, she uses her voice to tell stories and encourage others to live out their individual stories to the fullest.

She has a B.A. degree from SUNY Buffalo State and is grateful to have worked with top Hollywood entertainment companies including Lionsgate and Summit Entertainment.

Danni lives to tell stories as an actress and to produce stellar content for her clients and loves that she can work alongside the love of her life and her AminoCat family.

She also loves being a mom to her beautiful daughter, and with a son on the way Danni and Jeff hope to raise their family to follow their biggest dreams.

INVITATION FROM THE AUTHOR

I would love to connect with you to help you share your story. If you have a vision for yourself, your brand, or product that you'd love to bring to life through video, let's make it happen!

CONNECT WITH THE AUTHOR

Business Name: AminoCat Entertainment
Website: www.aminocat.com
Email: danni@aminocat.com

You are bigger, much
bigger, than any adversity
that comes your way.

Ladan Burroughs

Sometimes the very gift you were born with, your divine character, the very thing that gives you a sense of accomplishment, is the same thing that life seems to attack. I was born in Iran to two well-to-do parents. My mom, a highly motivated and educated Persian woman, and my dad, an American who rose from poverty into someone who worked with Iran's Shah. My parents truly lived a full life; fear did not hinder them from any experience or accomplishment.

In 1971, I was a spirited three-year-old. I would climb up tall trees and was often found walking on top of the ten-foot-high brick wall that surrounded our house. One day, my nanny and I were walking from our house to the pizza parlor. While we walked a man all in black—black helmet, dressed in black leather with heavy black motorcycle boots—started following us. I was clinging to my nanny. She picked me up and whispered in my ear, "If you don't listen to me, I will have him take you away, so you better start listening to me well." Did she know this guy? Was this threat just for the moment or forever? This experience was so embedded into me that this spirit of fear—no, terror—that was spoken into me became my constant companion for many years to come.

Before the revolution, life in Iran was majestic. My friend, fear, was not my constant companion; he didn't reign over my life. He would just throw little reminders in like, "Are you really going to walk to the store around the corner? You know there are lots of kidnappers that like to take little girls." An attack on your divine character is countered by another gift which gives you the strength to reach your full potential. Some called my character quality, stubborn, but I call it, persistent. I would feel the fear, my heart pounding. I was aware of every car and person that drove by. Just like the direction app that recalculates when you take a wrong turn, my brain would recalculate an escape route with every change in my environment. But it didn't stop me from going down to the store.

Every year my family would go to London for summer vacation, then continue to the United States and stop in the South of France before returning to Iran for the new school year. It was the summer of 1979. We were in Nice for Bastille Day. The beauty of the French Riviera beaches would have been enough but add the fireworks and the food, and the atmosphere was divine. Then the news came; the religious Khomeini was to return to Iran after being exiled. That was the start of the revolution. Maybe we should not have returned. Return we did, and that changed my whole life.

When we returned, Iran was like a war zone. There were curfews, machine guns, a shortage of food, images of executions and shootings. A dark foreboding blanket had fallen over the country. I'm not sure why my parents, as educated as they were, felt that life for me should continue as normal, but they did. Oftentimes I was the only child on the school bus. Most parents either kept their children home or drove them personally to school. One day, as we were going to school, the revolutionaries, as they were called, declared a curfew. Typically, curfews were at sundown. This one was during the early part of the day. While I was still on the bus to school they started with the machine gun fire. They were shooting up into the air but being in a school bus with the guns going off and the glass trembling around me was still frightening. I remember crouching between the seats hoping not to get hit by stray bullets.

Then, my dad had to flee the country. The revolutionary guards were looking for him as he had been accused of being a CIA agent. He has recorded his own story in a memoir, but this is my story. The guards burst through the door to our newly rented apartment asking for "the American". My mom answered them in Farsi and said there is no American, and that was true. I was so afraid that they would ask me a question. Even though I was born and raised in Iran, I had an American accent when I spoke Farsi. I turned my face towards the wall, pulled the covers tightly around my neck and pretended to be sleeping. I feared that if they knew I was half American they would take me away to prison, which meant certain death and torture.

After that experience, my mom realized that we were in danger and it would be a matter of time before they connected my dad to us. I was not told that we would be moving to the United States, but that we were going to visit for Christmas. The night before we left, I walked in to say goodnight and caught my mom and my dad's secretary rolling up $1000 bills and placing them in a cigarette case. In those days the cigarette cases opened like a big Tic Tac dispenser. When I questioned my mom about what they were doing, she told me that she was taking money out of the country because of the revolution. She told me that when we were at the airport I was not to acknowledge anyone that I knew and to keep my mouth shut as life and death depended on it. The new government had strict limits on the amount of cash and assets one person could take out of the country. We would have to live on what she was able to smuggle out and she had enlisted a few friends to carry out some of our family's assets.

I kept a keen eye on the cigarette case as it was moved from her handbag to her suitcase and back to her purse depending on what security line we were in. My face must have been blue because with every move of the cigarette case I would hold my breath. I was sure those same guards with the bayonets were going to come find us at the airport. I was sure I was going to die and be tortured. The movie *Argo* accurately depicts the suspense and apprehension I felt. I held my breath as we boarded the plane and felt the suffocation of fear as we waited to take off.

The tension on the plane was tangible. I am sure we were not the only people with a secret. Whether it was a cigarette packet, a diamond hidden in chewing gum (don't swallow) or other creative methods of smuggling out assets. Once we left the airspace of Iran and the airlines were allowed to serve alcohol, the passengers cheered. I could not believe how quickly they started drinking. I did not feel any relief until I heard the words, "We are approaching landing at Heathrow Airport." I took my first full breath and fell asleep. We were one step closer to our destination. We would stay with my uncle for a while who lived an hour north of San Francisco. I knew I would be safe. I wondered what this new life would bring. After Christmas break I started school in the United States. Maybe it was the culture shock, the new way of life, or maybe I was still numb from my experience, but I did not feel my terror companion with me. Maybe I had left him behind in Iran.

I got married to my high school sweetheart, a tall, strong, and athletic man. I felt very protected. Then he changed professions and became a Law Enforcement Officer. I don't know if it was the stories he told, the guns we owned, or just the fact that he worked at night and I was by myself, but my fear returned with a vengeance. We had purchased a condominium with a small skylight in the middle. Alone at night, I could not walk under that skylight because I was sure a man with a machine gun would jump down and get me. I knew this was irrational—a man would barely fit through the skylight. But even during the day I would glance up to make sure no one was there. I assumed everyone lived with this kind of fear, though somewhere deep down I realized this might not be normal.

A year or so after the heightened reemergence of my fear, my marriage ended. I found myself alone every night. I was in emotional pain and feared for my financial survival. I was working full-time for a local government office, but I did not make enough to meet all my obligations. I decided to get a second job at a retail store in the customer service department which meant I would get home late at night to an empty house. At least I hoped the house was empty. My new condominium had an assigned carport. As soon as I would park my car my heart would start beating fast and dread would overtake me. But my persistence in wanting to live a normal life was greater than the panic that took over my body. I have often wondered if someone watching me would have known what was happening inside of me.

I created a routine for the nights I got home late. First, I would have my keys ready to go so I would not be delayed at the door. I would get out of the car and look around the carport to make sure there was no one there. I would scan the hedges and the bush next to the front door—the perfect places for someone to be hiding. The bush by the door triggered my imagination worst of all. Have you heard the saying, "She sees a demon behind every bush"? My fear was that someone could jump out and drag me off. Or worse, they would push their way into the house. Once in the house, I would lock the door then proceed to check the closets and the bathrooms to make sure no intruder was hiding. This was my nightly routine. By the end of it I was exhausted.

Even though I had promised myself I would never remarry, I did. If there is a higher level of fear than terror, I found it when I had kids. I always had a large freezer stuffed full of food. I did not want them to ever feel hungry. I was so afraid that a kidnapper would take them that I would lock the windows at night in a two-story house with no air-conditioning in 100 degree weather.

My best friend and I would meet every Wednesday night. She was the only one who really knew the depths of all my struggles. She knew how terror would permeate every part of my life. We were both working moms. She, as a civil engineer, made too much money to quit, and I never wanted anyone to decide my financial future or have that sort of control over me. At our Wednesday night meetings we would talk, encourage, and pray for each other.

One Wednesday night we stayed out until the restaurant closed. As soon as I got in my car and left the comfort of my friend I began dreading the routine of getting in the house. As I approached the gate I made sure the doors were locked. I looked to either side to make sure no one was hiding in the ditch or behind the tree. Reason would argue that he would have to be super skinny to hide behind the tree, but fear and reason don't always get along. Most of the time I could reason the unreasonableness of the fear and keep going. But not tonight; I couldn't get out of the car. I was stuck to the seat and could not move. I wasn't sure what to do. I couldn't stay in the car all night, but I was afraid to leave it. I felt trapped. I decided to call my husband, who was asleep in bed, to come and open the gate for me. He came without any discussion and helped me inside. I never wanted to inconvenience anyone because of my problem and I never asked him after that.

Fear and terror were sneaky and hungry. They seemed to want more and more of me. Fear for my children's futures, fear of being homeless, fear of not being accepted, fear of not being good enough...

One day, an old friend, Sean, came over to introduce his new wife. During dinner, he looked at me and said, "I see a spirit of fear all over you. Can I pray for you after dinner?" I did not think much of it at the time, but I said yes. He was an old resident of the property I lived on. We used to hang out and talk. Why was he just seeing my fear now? After the kids were settled in he said, "Let's go into the kitchen and I will pray for you." I had no idea what was about to happen. He started with a standard prayer in English. Then he said he was going to pray in a warrior language. He must have prayed for over an hour. I had no idea what he was saying, until one moment I felt it. My old friend, this thing that was in me, the man in black, finally released me. Or maybe I released him, but just like that he was gone. Twenty years of men behind bushes, men with machine guns standing on the skylight, terror at my own front door. Gone. The feeling was peaceful, empty, calm, invigorated, free. I had no love for the man in black, but I felt the empty space he used to occupy. Sean walked into my home twenty-two years ago, prayed for me and walked out. I have not seen him since.

• • •

Today I have four sons and one daughter. I am proud of each one of them. They each possess gifts different from mine that I love and appreciate. They are all growing and taking on life in their own way. I have confidence in them and their abilities. They are my delight. I am sure my fears have had some effect on them, but I hope they are minimal. Freedom from fear allows me to accept the path my children take in life.

I bought a payroll firm almost eight years ago. I have since transformed it into a hub that offers many more services and works hard to see the community around it succeed. When I bought the business, I continued to provide payroll services to existing clients, but soon new small businesses started coming on board. Then, these businesses began asking for other services. They said we provided the peace of mind they needed to grow. I added more services to my firm's practice, including full charge bookkeeping, management, and compliance. As I became more involved with clients and saw recommendations come in, I understood that I was watching a community coming together. Business owners from all backgrounds were working with me on growing their businesses.

I believe it is because of my experiences, and my conquest over fear, that I have been able to connect with other business owners in a unique way. I'm grateful for the trust I've built with my community and the relationships that have flourished. For me, success has always been a team sport. I have chosen to use my strength to strengthen other business owners; I thrive on watching others succeed. I have chosen the area of finance, specifically bookkeeping, payroll, management, and compliance, to help business owners thrive.

I pray that my story will encourage you to seek out what is important to you in your life, that you will be stubborn and persistent enough to keep at your dreams. I also hope you will remember that someone seemingly insignificant may enter your life for a brief moment and send you in a direction that brings you success.

Be firm. Be kind. You never know what someone is dealing with.

And remember: a rising tide raises all ships.

LADAN BURROUGHS

Ladan Burroughs is an experienced businesswoman with a successful payroll and bookkeeping firm in the Bay Area of California.

Her story is one of courage, growth, and conquest in which she overcame the many obstacles that materialized throughout her life. From a terrifying experience in her home country of Iran to becoming a thriving business owner, Ladan has transformed the community around her for the better.

She began her entrepreneurial journey with a small payroll company and, before she knew it, Ladan had formed connections with countless small businesses, assisting them in their development and everyday operations.

Ladan continues to expand her influence and takes great pride in the positive change her community has seen over the past several years.

INVITATION FROM THE AUTHOR

Want to free up your time and get peace of mind around your book-keeping and payroll? Connect with me to learn about how my business can help yours!

CONNECT WITH THE AUTHOR

Business name: LB Business Solutions
Website: www.ladanburroughs.com/
Facebook: www.facebook.com/LBBsolutions
Email: ladan@ladanburroughs.com

A relationship needs a vision; two people looking in the same direction and supporting each other's passions. It demands attention; making your partner the most important person in your universe. And it requires courage; being ready to step into the unknown to grow stronger together.

Alise Axelsson

It's 2016 and I am taking my regular route back home from work. It is a cold winter day. My head is full of thoughts. As the subway doors open, I step out and the sounds of the street above tumbles down the stairs towards me. The station is only a couple hundred meters from my apartment. Usually, I hurry to get home. Today, I walk incredibly slowly. I don't want to go home to my husband and my one-year-old son. Am I crazy?

I take out my phone and with shaking hands I write to my husband, "Hi baby, I had a tough day at work. I'll go for a short walk before I come up, ok?"

His reply comes very quickly. "Of course, whatever you need."

And as I pass my apartment I cannot help but feel guilt and shame—for not speaking the truth and for failing my own self. But I keep moving forward. And with every step I take I can't help but feel how lost I am. I married the man I loved, but I am not happy. I can't remember the last time we made love passionately. I can't think of a recent conversation we had that would lead to deep connection and love. And the more I think about it the lonelier I feel. And then there's my job. I've worked so hard to get it, but now I am not happy there either. And I can't help but ask the question: How did I end up here?

And as I walk down the road, I feel my right hand slipping into my pocket and reaching for my phone. I unlock it and my mind guides me to look for inspiration. Anything that would help me to see through this. Anything that would give me a hint as to what my next step should be. And there it is. I see a video with a title that speaks to my heart. I click on it and the speaker's encouraging words and calming voice makes me want to listen more and more. As I listen to it my mind calms down. With every word it feels like the author speaks about my life. It's like he knows me. And for the first time I immerse myself fully. I allow the words and the music to guide me to a place where I will know what to do. I'm thirty minutes into the video and my inner voice says, "If anyone is going to change your life, it will be you." I stop in my tracks. And the voice continues. "Yes. If anyone is going to change your life, it will be you." The same words keep repeating in my head until I get home.

When I open my apartment door, I know exactly what needs to be done. I drop my bag and I look for my son. More than anything I just want to hug him. I see my husband. He is sitting on the couch. And I feel that part of him that loves me unconditionally. I feel his loving heart and I melt in the kindness of his eyes. But there is also another part of him that I see for the first time. A part of him that is hurting which I never saw before. Not because he wasn't showing it, but because I was simply too busy being stuck in my own thoughts that I never realized how much it hurt him to see me suffering. I take a seat next to him. I want to apologize, yet I don't know where to start.

"I listened to a video while I was out walking," I begin.

"What kind of video?" he asks.

"It was about taking responsibility for your own life. I have spent so much time thinking about what I don't have and what is missing in my life. I was blaming you for not being the husband I needed, I was blaming work, I was blaming my family for not supporting me enough. Listening to this video, I realized that everything in my life is already perfect. And now, for me to enjoy it and take it in, I need to learn how to be with myself. How to love and accept myself. How to be kind to myself. And how to trust myself."

"And I found this course that can help me to have the right start," I continue. I take out my phone to show him the program.

As soon as he sees the program, he says: "I know a friend who's working at that event."

"You do?" I ask while leaning more and more towards him.

"Yes," he says. "Let's call her now."

Excitement is starting to tingle in my stomach. Just an hour ago I felt hopeless and now I am taking action. As my husband hangs up the phone he turns towards me.

"She'll help you with the ticket."

"Thank you," I whisper, loud enough for my husband to hear. And no more words need to be said. We have connected again.

• • •

"The outside world mirrors our inner world. Change must begin from within."

— ALISE AXELSSON

It's been three months since the course and it feels like a lot has changed. My days are filled with joy and happiness. I enjoy spending more time with my family. I am calm. And for the first time I have started to take care of myself. I have my own time, I exercise, I meet my friends more often, and I have even thought about starting my own business. It's been a while since I felt interest and passion for my job. And I have been feeling that change is coming. I am just waiting for a sign.

It's early morning, and I am sitting at my workplace surrounded by the sounds of frantic typing, people chattering everywhere, and the blare of office lights. I am nervous. This day is not like other days. There is a part of me that already knows that after today my life will be different.

My heart starts to beat faster as I watch my boss rise from his chair. He turns around and looks at me, and I know it's time for our meeting. As the door closes behind me I can tell by the look on his face that he's not here to deliver happy news. And there it is. He announces that my department is being restructured and my position is no longer available. I have to hide the happiness inside. For two years I have wanted to leave my job. I was always worried about finding another job and I doubted whether it was the right decision. But even at this moment, with all the questions running through my mind, I know it's a clear sign that my time here is done. Someone is making the decision for me as I didn't have the guts to do it myself. And just like that, a ten-year-long relationship has ended.

The clock on the wall hits 5:00 p.m. as I walk out of the building. I stop to spend a couple minutes on the staircase leading down to the street. I close my eyes and I take a deep breath. I don't know what I will do or what will be the next step for me yet, but I feel so incredibly free.

. . .

"You are exactly where you need to be in your life. Even if it's painful and scary. Because there is something you need to learn and realize here to become a better version of yourself."

— ALISE AXELSSON

"I understand, thank you so much for calling me," I say gently and hang up the phone.

That was the fifth job interview this week and still no progress. Either I am too qualified for the position or I don't have the experience needed. I was certain that finding another job would be easy. Yet, three months have passed and all I have done is send out CV's and take calls that tell me, "I'm sorry, we have chosen someone else." And the more time I spend at home, the more challenges arise in my relationship. I get upset when he works too much. And even though I know that I help by taking care of the house, I don't feel appreciated. I don't feel like I am doing something important.

But there's one thing bothering me even more. Since I lost my job, he has been supporting me financially. And when I was young I dreamed about being with a man who would support me and take care of me. Now it's happening, but I'm not happy. And the worst part is, I'm ready to take jobs I don't want just to regain my financial independence. What is the matter with me? Somewhere I know something deep is hidden, but I don't have the answer to it yet.

Another month has passed and still no job. But today I care less. I am busy packing our suitcases. I have been longing for this day to come.

While I was at the event in spring, I bought two more tickets to another event that starts tomorrow. This time I'm not going alone. My husband is traveling with me. We've spent all our money and borrowed more to be able to go to this course. Our relationship has been going through a challenging time, and we know we need help. So, today we are flying across the world to spend six days facing our deepest fears, individually and as a couple. And even though I feel nervous, I am so looking forward to it. I am ready.

Six days flies by like a blink of an eye. We are supposed to be flying home today but our flight has been cancelled until tomorrow. We stay at a hotel overnight. It has beautiful views over Miami beach. It's a gorgeous day. I wish I could just run outside and roll around in the warm sun-kissed sand and dive into the water, but I cannot get out of bed. The event was intense. Very little sleep, lots of emotions, untold stories of truth. I faced fears that nearly crushed me.

I force myself to go down to the beach. I lay down on a towel, close my eyes and just listen to the sound of the waves. And as I listen to the water as it smashes against the coast, I drift back into the memories of recent events. I have learned so many things. But what resonated with me the most was the course's lessons about polarity.

Since I was a child, I've loved watching thunder. I always wondered what was behind the power of those booming roars. Thunder sounds when opposite poles collide. Relationships are no different. When feminine and masculine energy comes together, it creates thunder. Nothing is more powerful than attraction between these two poles. But so far, I have been afraid to show my thunder. I have been afraid of seeing and accepting myself as I am. I have lived with the illusion that

I will get hurt if I open my heart to him. But I didn't realize that I was already hurting, living with the fear of not being enough.

I am determined to change this. And just by making this decision, my husband and I have reconnected. And for the first time I feel that I am ready to let go of my "macho" attitude—of always striving to be strong and independent. I never knew that I had put up that protective mask because I was afraid of being hurt. But I want to learn how to be vulnerable. I want to learn how to show my emotions without feeling weak. I want to learn how it feels to be taken care of, to be treated like a queen. I want to learn how to put myself first without feeling guilty. And I start by telling my husband that I will stop looking for jobs. I want to give him more space in our relationship and allow him to take care of me. And I will also follow my heart and start my own company. It's an instant relief.

We have arrived home. I purchase a coaching program while drinking my morning coffee. I have decided to become a relationship coach. This last year has been transformational in so many ways, for myself and my relationship, and I want to help other couples to create deep connection, intimacy, and passion in their relationship.

I spend every day studying. I watch tutorials. I reflect on my own relationship. I test different techniques and, step by step, the relationship between me and my husband improves. We are in love again. It's exciting to be together. With every day we get closer. And for the first time in a long time I am happy.

Five months into the program I gain my first clients. I offer two coaching sessions in exchange for a testimonial from the client. I find I enjoy working with people and start to receive positive feedback. It feels incredible to see these powerful transformations my clients go through. I start organizing small events for couples, teaching them how to create a passionate relationship. I have spent the last few weeks reaching out to people in my network and marketing my upcoming event. I arrive an hour before the event at the small conference room. I walk back and forth trying to memorize the script I am planning to share with the audience. I have a list of twenty attendees in front of me and as the time gets closer and closer I cannot help but look out the doors to see if anyone is coming. The first person I see coming down the hall is my husband. But there's no one else. Suddenly, I hear footsteps approaching the conference room. It's one of the guests, my best friend. I welcome them and show them around, but I cannot hide the disappointment inside. None of the other guests come.

Three weeks later I am in another conference room. An even better presentation, more content, and more value, I think to myself. I have spent days preparing. It's a bigger room and I expect more people to show up. I patiently wait in the hall to welcome the guests, but no one is here. This time two people arrive out of the twenty-five on the list.

I come home convinced that I need to buy a course or hire a person that will teach me how to find the right people for my events. I invest in several programs, I start my own platform, and I start running my own webinars. I put in a lot of hard work to make it happen. And while I'm doing preparations, one thought keeps spinning in my head: Are my programs too expensive? I halved the price for the last event, but no one came.

By now, I have spent all my savings to pay for the rent of different locations, and since I haven't sold any of my programs I have no money to reinvest. Frustrated, I ask my husband for financial support to organize another event.

Three weeks later I am standing in a room that is filling up with people. Hearing people talking and laughing makes me happy. More than twenty women have come to my seminar. This time I increase the prices and am confident I'll close the deals. Everything goes well until I get to the selling part. Before I even start to explain the offer, I have already discounted the price in my head thinking it's too expensive. Then I added a couple of extra sessions and gifts to make sure the offer looks really packed. And while I present, I keep on adding free gifts. I feel so disconnected with myself. I speak too fast, saying words I was not planning to say. They all love the seminar, but no one buys a package.

I come home and collapse on the couch. I can't hold back my devastation. Tears just keep coming. In my head I go over and over what I did wrong. My husband hears me crying from another room and he comes to me.

"What's wrong?" He asks.

"I didn't sell anything," I say. "I don't think this is what I should be doing. I think I should just go back to my corporate job, where at least I was good at something."

"Look at me," my husband interrupts. "I think you are amazing at what you do, and it breaks my heart to see you this way. When will you stop doubting yourself?"

Great question, I think.

The next morning, while having breakfast, my phone rings. It's one of my best friends. I pick up the phone and I hear her happy voice. I have been following her for a while on social media. She has built her business after years of struggle and now has an avalanche of clients. She asks me how my business is going.

"It's tough," I say quietly.

"Listen, I know what the problem is," she says.

"You do?"

"The reason why my business took off is because I discovered something. And you need it too. Now!"

The next day we meet for coffee and she tells me about a coach she met a year ago. At that time, she had been single for eight years and was desperate to finally meet someone. Her coach told her the solution to this eight-year hiatus. They explained that there were self-sabotaging beliefs in her subconscious mind that kept attracting the wrong type of men. She could change it all by reprogramming her mind.

And while I listen to her story my jaw slowly drops. This is all new to me. But it begins to make sense.

"So, did she help you with your business?" I ask my friend.

"No," she replies. "She helped me to meet the love of my life."

"What about your business?" I keep asking.

"I invented my own method," she says. "And for the last six months I have been working on removing subconscious blocks within myself and it has brought incredible results."

She doesn't need to tell me more. At that point, I am ready to do whatever it takes to work with her. And from that day I become her client.

The next six months are the most magical yet painful in my life. It is magical because I have never felt so confident and certain about who I am and what I have to offer. It is painful because going through sessions with my coach brings up childhood trauma, reliving how my parents always fought, how we lived in poverty. I thought that I had moved past those challenges since they happened twenty years ago. But I didn't know that subconsciously they were still there. All those programs of low self-worth, low self-confidence, fear of judgement and rejection, fear of failure, were always sabotaging me while presenting and selling, leaving me paralyzed and playing it small. And while I thought that I was helping people by making my services more affordable, in reality I was selling my own fear. But fear can only attract more fear. It cannot attract abundance.

The moment I start to work on increasing my self-worth, everything changes. And with every session I become freer, more confident, happier and it begins to reflect in my life and my business. At my first event after the program I sell my coaching packages for five times more than my corporate salary. I don't spend days preparing, I don't discount anything, I don't add extra sessions or gifts while presenting. It's a completely different game. I have changed, and that change is reflecting in my business.

A couple of months later, my friend invites me over for dinner. By the look on her face, I can tell that there is something she wants to tell me.

"Would you like to be partners?" she asks. My eyes grow wider.

"Partners?" I ask.

"Would you like to work together?" she asks more intensely.

"Yes!" I say. I couldn't be happier.

All these incredible things in my life started from the moment I made a decision to change my life.

• • •

From the day I started to take on my first clients, I have had the privilege of meeting and working with so many extraordinary women. Seeing them heal their pain and find their way back to their true selves is what makes my work meaningful. And once they regain their true power everything changes. They are able to create deeper and more meaningful connections with their partners. When they are able to fully trust and open up to their partners they experience more intimacy and passion. And once they learn how to truly love and appreciate themselves, the world becomes their oyster. They are finally one with themselves again. And everything they touch blossoms.

If you are in a place right now where you feel stuck and don't know what your next step should be, or you know you deserve so much more but you cannot see what you need to change to get there, I know exactly how you feel. I know how overwhelming it might be. But all you need to do is to decide that the time to create a life of your dreams is now. The time to create the relationship you have always wanted is now.

You don't need any plans or strategies. You just need to begin with a decision. And once you make this brave choice, I guarantee you that your life will change. The right path will show up for you and you will know what to do.

ALISE AXELSSON

Alise Axelsson is recognized as one of Sweden's leading relationship experts. She has transformed the lives of hundreds of people through her live events and programs.

Her career took a steep hike after founding the Stellar Coaching Academy and beginning her work with the "Wealth Decoded" method, helping people to remove their self-limiting subconscious beliefs and showing them how to create relationships filled with intimacy and passion.

Alise is a certified relationship coach. Her passion for working with people and helping them to create lasting love in their intimate relationships came into her life more than five years ago, when she felt a desperate need for guidance in her own intimate relationship.

Alise also holds a bachelor's degree in international business. Her background is in the banking industry where she worked as foreign exchange trader for many years.

Apart from being a successful business woman, she is a wife to an incredible man and a mother to two amazing children. She loves nature and traveling. She is crazy about an active lifestyle, a tasty cup of coffee, and time together with friends and family.

INVITATION FROM THE AUTHOR

If you are ready to reignite passion, intimacy, and a deeper connection with your partner, I have a gift for you—my *3 Secrets to Lasting Love and Passion*. You can grab it here:

shorturl.at/cgpL1

CONNECT WITH THE AUTHOR

Business Name: Stellar Coaching Academy
Website: www.stellarcoach.se/
Facebook: www.facebook.com/alise.axelsson
Email: info@stellarcoach.se

MESSAGE FROM THE PUBLISHER

Back in 2020, I sent out the call for women everywhere to rise. My vision for this anthology series was to bring together women from around the world whose inspiring stories would ignite the female entrepreneurs of tomorrow. These were women who had rediscovered their purpose, brought their business ideas to fruition, and have found freedom and joy in living their best lives. I brought these women together to show the world that when women collaborate, we are an unstoppable force. That together, we are stronger. Three editions and forty-five powerful stories later, this journey has come to an end.

You have read the honest accounts from female entrepreneurs who have poured their hearts and souls into this book; their purpose, to share and inspire, and pave a better way for the women who will go after them. My hope is that there was something for everyone within these pages, and that at least one, if not all of these stories, might touch the lives of readers and create ripple effects of hope and change throughout our world.

I have loved bringing you these stories about failures and hardships, successes and wins. Everyone begins their journey with doubts and hurdles in their way. Whatever those doubts and hurdles, whether we have created them in our own minds, or they are placed before us by others, we take them head on, because we know there is something positive waiting for us.

To the women of the future, now it is your turn. Where will the course of your journey lead you? How will you make your dreams a reality? In short, what is your story? Because it is not over yet. I hope you will take this book and its stories with you; that the experiences and lessons learned will shine a light on the road ahead.

But at the heart of this book is a simple truth: trust in your own path. There is no other time or place you need to be right now, and there is no one else who can walk in your shoes. Trust in yourself and your abilities. You are enough. Seize every day, knowing you can make it. There is no better time than today to rise up for your tomorrow.

'When She Rises, She Rises with Tomorrow in mind. Even though she cannot see what the future holds, she knows if she takes action now there will be a positive outcome in the future. Her ideas and dreams will manifest into reality, and it all starts with her determination to rise!'

To your Success!

Kimmie Wong

www.ingramcontent.com/pod-product-compliance
Lightning Source LLC
Chambersburg PA
CBHW071650200326
41519CB00012BA/2470